A Woman in a War-Torn Town

The Journal of Jane Howison Beale
Fredericksburg, Virginia
1850–1862

About 1 o'clock there was a little cessation of the firing, and we heard my dear brother John's voice at the door, calling us to come while we could get out of the town, but when he came in and saw our condition he knew we could not walk, and get those poor sufferers past the danger in times, and after holding a hasty council with the other gentlemen it was judged too rash an undertaking for us to attempt, then, brother John told us that the town was on fire in many places, a whole row of buildings on Main St were already burnt; and as my house had a shingled roof I thought we would soon be driven from it by fire also Mr Lacy left us with brother John and they could scarcely have got out of the town before the heavy Bombardment commenced again and the sound of 173 guns ~~struck~~ in our ears, the shrieking of those shells, like a host of angry fiends rushing through the air, the crashing of the balls

A Woman in a War-Torn Town

The Journal of Jane Howison Beale
Fredericksburg, Virginia
1850–1862

Edited by Kerri S. Barile and Barbara P. Willis
Preface by Paula S. Felder
Introduction by John Hennessy with Barbara P. Willis

THE
DONNING COMPANY
PUBLISHERS

The text of *The Journal of Jane Howison Beale* was copied from the handwritten original, maintaining the idiosyncracies of Mrs. Beale's writing, including her spelling, abbreviations, and punctuation.

Unless otherwise stated, all images are from the files of HFFI, Fredericksburg, Virginia.

Copyright © 1979 and 2011 by Historic Fredericksburg Foundation, Inc.
1200 Caroline Street
Fredericksburg, VA 22401
www.hffi.org

The Donning Company Publishers
184 Business Park Drive, Suite 206
Virginia Beach, VA 23462

Steve Mull, *General Manager*
Barbara B. Buchanan, *Office Manager*
Richard A. Horwege, *Senior Editor*
Stephanie Danko, *Graphic Designer*
Priscilla Odango, *Imaging Artist*
Lori Porter, *Project Research Coordinator*
Tonya Washam, *Marketing Specialist*
Pamela Engelhard, *Marketing Advisor*

Dennis N. Walton, *Project Director*

Library of Congress Cataloging-in-Publication Data

Beale, Jane Howison, 1815–1882.
    [Journal of Jane Howison Beale, Fredericksburg, Virginia, 1850–1862]
    A woman in a war-torn town : the journal of Jane Howison Beale, Fredericksburg, Virginia, 1850–1862 / edited by Kerri S. Barile and Barbara P. Willis ; preface by Paula S. Felder ; introduction by John Hennessy with Barbara P. Willis.
        p.   cm.
    Includes bibliographical references and index.
    ISBN 978-1-57864-664-7 (softcover : alk. paper)
1. Beale, Jane Howison, 1815–1882—Diaries. 2. Fredericksburg (Va.)—Biography. 3. Women—Virginia—Fredericksburg—Diaries. 4. United States—History—Civil War, 1861–1865—Personal narratives, Confederate. 5. Virginia—History—Civil War, 1861–1865—Personal narratives. 6. Fredericksburg, Battle of, Fredericksburg, Va., 1862—Personal narratives. I. Barile, Kerri S. II. Willis, Barbara P. III. Title.
    F234.F8B39 2011
    975.5'36603092—dc22
    [B]
                                    2010050780

Printed in the USA at Walsworth Publishing Company

Contents

List of Illustrations

Preface
A BRAVE WOMAN FACES TRAGEDY AND WAR

"I love to see that lofty independence of character in woman which teaches her to rely upon herself in trying exigencies, particularly when it is accompanied by a refined sensibility." Thus did Jane Howison Beale, writing in the first year of widowhood in admiration of the courage of another, characterize the standard by which she herself lived.

In the spring of the year 1850, William, her beloved husband, died suddenly of a heart attack even as she lay a semi-invalid following the birth of their tenth child. They had married in 1833, she but nineteen and he an older widower; and their marriage had been a singularly happy one. Her loss was as total as her dependency on him had been.

On August 22, as she lay still recuperating from the birth of her son Samuel, her mother also was taken from her by illness. She was thus deprived of her chief source of comfort and left to rear and support nine small children alone (one child died in infancy).

After the loss of her mother, Jane Beale was driven to express her grief by keeping a diary, "for I have no bosom friend to sympathize in my deep sorrow now." What sustained her over the next months of pain and loneliness were her deep religious faith, the love and support of a close-knit family and friends, and a talent for writing.

What began as an outlet for her grief soon turned into a therapeutic commentary—on her own feelings and on the world around her. Before a month was out, she was writing instinctively to an audience. "I will here digress to introduce this pair, to whom? Why to themselves if they should perchance get hold of these pages."

Over the ensuing months her passages on pain and sorrow were increasingly intermingled with livelier comments. She followed national events as well as the comings and goings of her large family. She loved her sisters with deep affection and was proud of her brothers. She grew anxious about the hardships awaiting her children. "The world with all its interests seems to occupy a smaller space and to be of far less value than it formerly appeared." She was closest to the happiness she had once known "when the family party assembles around the bright lamplight in the evening."

On April 22, 1851, the first anniversary of William Beale's death, she relived in her journal the last day of his life. This catharsis seemed to release her energies for her own present, and soon afterward she gave up writing in her journal for several years.

In January 1854, as if prompted by a New Year's resolution, Jane resumed writing, but her sole entry for the year seemed more of a progress report to posterity than a private communion with her thoughts. There followed a similar entry in 1855. And by January 1856, she was reduced to writing about the weather. For a time, the journal had outgrown its usefulness and she her need for it.

Five years later, the tragedy and drama of war and her own patriotic excitement caused her to resume her writing, just as it had been her outlet for her intense feelings some years earlier. In 1861, after the Battle of Manassas, she made several emotional entries in the journal.

But, it was the year 1862, when the people of Fredericksburg came to know war firsthand (and she lost her son Charles in battle), that roused her to record a detailed account of the drama. The climax of her story comes at the Battle of Fredericksburg in December, when her family, unaware of the evacuation warning, was forced to spend a night of terror under bombardment before being rescued by her brother. The journal ends with her return to the plundered town to find "with strange and glad surprise" that her home and its belongings were safe.

Jane's narrative as a participant/observer during these traumatic months accounts for more than half of the little handwritten volume which has been passed down since her death in 1882. Her diary would do credit to a professional journalist, and one cannot escape the impression that she would be proud to have it read.

Paula S. Felder
Preface to the Fourth Edition, 1995

Acknowledgments

The first edition of *The Journal of Jane Howison Beale* was published by the Historic Fredericksburg Foundation, Inc., in 1979 under the direction of Barbara P. Willis. The first edition and subsequent incarnations were greatly aided by the efforts of Barbara P. Willis, Paula S. Felder, Mary Eva Repass, Sue Hintz, Ronald Shibley, and Catharine J. Farley.

Like previous versions, this fifth edition of the journal would not have been possible without the support of many people. The current volume was edited by Kerri S. Barile, vice president of HFFI, and Barbara P. Willis, Fredericksburg historian. They were assisted in this endeavor by the HFFI Publications Committee: Kerri Barile (chair), Linda Bellard, Carthon Davis III, Jeffrey Edmunds, John Hennessy, Loretta Lettner, Jerrilynn Eby MacGregor, Sean Maroney (HFFI executive director), Bill Shorter, Scott Walker, and Barbara P. Willis.

Lori Syner and Megan Higgins at HFFI painstakingly converted the typed manuscript into an electronic format to bring the journal text into the "modern age." Current photographs of Beale-related places were taken by Kerri Barile, Carthon Davis III, and Sean Maroney, executive director. Civil War period images were collected by John Hennessy, past president of the organization and chief historian for the Fredericksburg and Spotsylvania National Military Park. The City of Fredericksburg graciously provided the current base map used to illustrate the places notable to Jane in the Introduction section.

Great appreciation is also given to the Fredericksburg Area Museum and Cultural Center, especially Mary Helen Dellinger, curator, for allowing HFFI to photograph the journal for this edition, and, moreover, for ensuring the long-term preservation of the journal itself.

Notes on Fredericksburg people and places were created by Barbara P. Willis, and war-related endnotes were crafted by local Civil War experts.

This book would not have been published without the aid of Miss Mary Graham Howison and Mrs. Wallace Stephens of "Braehead" who knew the location of the journal and furnished the organization with an abundance of information on the Howison and Beale families.

Most of all, grateful appreciation is given to Mrs. Charles F. Blue, Jr., of Charlottesville, Virginia, direct descendant of Jane Beale, who donated the original journal to the Historic Fredericksburg Foundation almost four decades ago. ▪

Introduction

by John Hennessy with Barbara P. Willis

Diaries are, perhaps, the most intimate and immediate of all historical records. While letters share the advantage of immediacy, they are invariably written for another's consumption. But diaries are often written for the soul of the writer, usually without regard for an ultimate reader. Indeed, in our society, reading someone's diary is the ultimate invasion of privacy.

While the musings of most diarists would not interest many beyond their immediate circle, a few carry meaning of broader import, containing first-person perspectives on our larger community and telling the stories—the trials, tragedies, and triumphs—of those places. Such is the case of Jane Beale's journal.

UNEARTHING A TREASURE

There are always gems of our history waiting to be dug out from hidden places. They are never really lost, but instead tucked away in a safe, secure place, patiently awaiting discovery. Such was the fate of the diary of Jane Beale, undiscovered for 109 years, waiting to be unearthed.

The existence of such a diary was hinted at by Jane's historian brother, Robert Reid Howison, in his published works on Virginia's past. He did not call her out by name, but simply referred to her diary as, "the MS Journal of a Fredericksburg lady I am under special obligation. . . ." It is not known exactly why the journal authoress remained nameless. Perhaps Robert's vague reference was intended as a brotherly shield to protect the privacy of his sister and her family; or, perhaps prevailing Victorian attitudes regarding women dissuaded him from identifying the source. Regardless, the Jane Beale journal and its author rested in obscurity, hidden from the academic world for the better part of a century.

It took the sleuthing of another young and enthusiastic "Fredericksburg lady" to bring the diary—and the identity of its author—out in the open. By the early 1970s, the Historic Fredericksburg Foundation, Inc. (HFFI) was over twenty years old. The venerable organization was looking for ways to bring history to the community and re-energize the spirits of history-minded residents and visitors. The HFFI Junior

Board went to work. They developed a tour guide service, opened a museum dedicated to Fredericksburg's history at what is today known as The Chimneys on Caroline Street, and established itself as a publishing venue for local historical material. One of the most active members of the Junior Board was Barbara Pratt Willis, an area native with an avid interest in, and immense talent for, researching the history of the Rappahannock River region. It was Barbara who rediscovered Robert Reid Howison's cryptic note about the existence of the journal and took it upon herself to uncover the whereabouts of the manuscript. As Barbara herself recounts:

> *My job as chair of the History and Research committee was to write the script for the tour guides. Reading the resources on local history, I came across references to "MS Journal of a Fredericksburg Lady." Deciding that this journal could be a key exhibit in the new museum plus a candidate for publication I became a sleuth. I was rewarded by knocking on the door of "Braehead," the historic home of the Howison family, which was occupied by sisters Miss Mary Graham Howison and Mrs. Nan Howison Wallace, granddaughters of historian Robert Reid Howison. These charming and erudite ladies not only knew that the author of the journal was their great-aunt Jane Howison Beale but also that the Journal had been passed down to their cousin, Mrs. Charles F. Blue, Jr., who lived in Charlottesville. I contacted Mrs. Blue on behalf of HFFI asking permission to display and publish the journal of her ancestor. In September 1972, Mrs. Blue graciously donated the original journal to HFFI.*

The Journal of Jane Howison Beale was first published by HFFI in 1979. The Foundation later donated the book to what is today the Fredericksburg Area Museum and Cultural Center to be placed on permanent display. Jane's journal stands as one of the best accounts of life in a small Southern town during the 1850s and early 1860s. It provides a glimpse into the life of one woman—a woman who represents many single mothers just like herself—struggling in an ever-changing world.

JANE AND HER LIFE

Jane Howison Beale was born Jane Briggs Howison in 1815, one of twelve children of Samuel and Helen Moore Howison. The family home, known today as the St. James House, was a charming eighteenth-century dwelling on Charles Street in downtown Fredericksburg. The Howisons were prominent members of the Fredericksburg Presbyterian Church on Hanover Street.

The Howison/Beale Family Tree

Samuel Howison (1779–1845) m. Helen (Nellie) Rose Moore (1784–1850)

Children

1. William (1803–1849)
2. Neil MacCoul (1805–1848)
3. Anne (1807–1872) m. a. Capt. James Thorburn
                                b. Commodore Thomas Dornin
4. John (1809–1879) m. a. Anne Lee
                                b. Lucy Rawlings
5. Marion (1812–1868) m. Richard Sterling
6. **Jane Briggs (1815–1882) m. William C. Beale**
7. Helen Mary (1817–1865) m. Capt. Robert Thorburn
8. James (1818– ?) m. Sallie Murry
9. Robert Reid (1820–1906) m. Mary Elizabeth Graham
10. Samuel Scott (1825–1885) m. Ann Ficklen
11. Edward Moore (Ned)
12. Elizabeth, died in infancy

William Beale of Fauquier Co. m. Hannah Gordon

Children

1. John
2. Sally m. Henry Cooke
3. Lucy m. Dr. John Esten Cooke
4. **William Churchill** m. a. Susan Vowels
                                son G. Douglass
                                dau. Mary m. James Linsay Gordon
                                dau. Eliza m. Reuben Linsay Gordon
                        ***b. Jane Briggs Howison**
5. Richard
6. Charles m. Mary Harrison Gordon
7. Edward
8. James

William Churchill Beale (1791–1850) m. 1834 Jane Briggs Howison (1815–1882)

*Children

1. Helen Gordon (1834–1883)
2. Lucy Cooke (1836–1898) m. a. John C. Brent
                                b. Frederick Page
3. William Coalter (1838–1877) m. Rebecca Clark
4. John Howison (1840–1868)
5. Charles Dornin (1842–1862)
6. Robert Cecil (1844–1911) m. Mammie Dornin
7. James McDonald (1845–1846) died in infancy
8. Marion Sterling (1847–1936) m. Francis Dunnington
9. Edward Julian (1848–1894)
10. Samuel Howison (1850–1913) m. Sallie Ann Scott

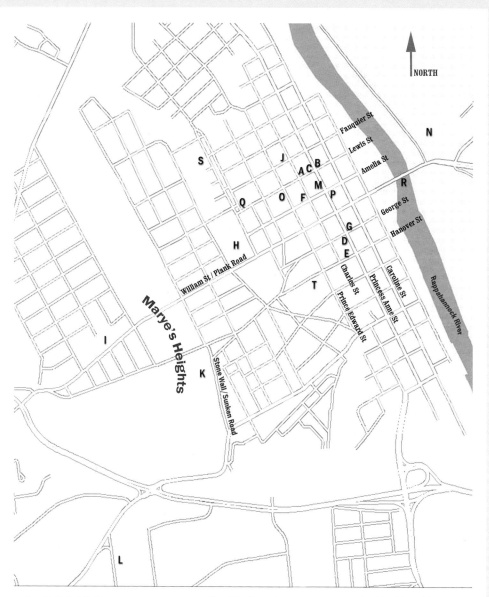

A= Jane Beale House
B= Knox House
C= Lomax House
D= Presbyterian Church
E= Carmichael House
F= McGuire House
G= St. George's Episcopal Church

H= City Cemetery
I = Rose Hill Farm
J = St. James House
K= Brompton
L= Braehead
M= Broaddus House
N= Chatham/Lacy House

O= Bankhead House
P= Baptist Church
Q = Kenmore
R= Chatham Bridge
S= Mary Washington
   Monument
T= Federal Hill

Jane Beale's Fredericksburg. (*Base map courtesy of the City of Fredericksburg*)

In 1834, at age nineteen, Jane married William Churchill Beale, a forty-three-year-old widower who was twenty-four years her senior. The Beale family first took up residence in a brick house near the Rappahannock River in the nearby town of Falmouth. In 1846, William Beale, by then a successful merchant, purchased a brick home at 307 Lewis Street in Fredericksburg and moved his family into the spacious thirty-year-old house located within a block of Jane's childhood home.

While her marriage brought Jane security, much love, and a burgeoning family, it also brought the risk that invariably attended such spring/winter romance: in 1850, when Jane was just thirty-six, her husband William died of a sudden heart attack. Her husband's death left Jane with nine young children to raise alone, including one born months after William's death. Jane's grief stimulated her to start her journal, a place to record her most intimate thoughts.

To settle her husband's estate, the family sold their mill in nearby Falmouth, and Jane was able to remain in her home. After alleviating the threat of eviction, Jane wrote about her immense relief that her greatest fears had been averted, noting: "It is now certain that all the debts of the Estate will be paid and this has cheered me much."[1]

Her home secured and abetted by the confidences scribbled in her diary, Jane Beale battled through her grief and took up teaching to help make ends meet. An educated woman, Jane opened a school for girls in a now-demolished brick building in the yard of her house. Her advertisements for students would become an annual rite in Fredericksburg for the next three decades. She also supplemented her income by taking in boarders.

After the cataclysm of grief that attended her husband's death—faithfully recorded in the diary's first year—Beale's journaling would become sporadic through the 1850s (she left no entries for 1852, 1853, and 1857–1860). In 1861, crisis again prompted her to take up her pen and journal. On July 23, 1861, just two days after the first major battle of the Civil War at Manassas—in which her sons John and Charles tangentially participated as part of the 1st Virginia Infantry—she started writing, stopping only rarely until the guns had gone silent at Fredericksburg in mid-December 1862, when her diary abruptly ends. Perhaps she continued writing beyond that point, but if so, those volumes have not survived (we lament). Jane remained in her home on Lewis Street until her death in 1882. She was sixty-seven years old.

THE DIARIST AND THE AMERICAN CIVIL WAR

Thousands of towns across America went to war in 1861, sending their sons off to battle. But of all those towns, only a handful had war boomerang back upon them in violent form. Fredericksburg was one of these, and Jane Beale's diary is one of the best chronicles of any community caught amidst war. She offers not just narration, but perception—an eyewitness account of a town transformed by war—physically, culturally, and socially. She writes not with the impassioned outrage of her neighbor and teenager Lizzie Alsop, whose unpublished diary faithfully records her eloquent diatribes against all things Yankee and (emphatically) her fondness for all things Confederate. Nor does Jane have access to the privileged information available to fellow diarist Betty Herndon Maury, whose father served in the highest echelons of the Confederate military. Instead, she observed with maturity and a palpable calmness (with a few exceptions), but always with deep feeling and sincerity. Of all of Fredericksburg's diarists, Jane's is the most representative of the perspective of her neighbors, most revealing of an experience shared by most white residents of the town.

Jane Beale's recounting of her family's experience under fire and as refugees on December 11, 1862, has become well known and is often quoted. But her regular musings tell us much that is important about her community, its condition, and a society in a state of violent transition. Jane was a woman of the South, who prized "refinement" in men and saw it as the product of both womanly and religious influences.[2] But she was, by necessity and nature, an independent soul. "I love to see," she wrote, "that lofty independence of character in [a] woman which teaches her to rely on herself in trying exigencies, particularly when it is accompanied by a refined sensibility."

Her abhorrence of the menial tasks involved in maintaining a home made the adjustment to running a household by herself difficult. "My mind is not constituted to love it," she lamented, "but a strong sense of duty combined with an earnest desire to secure the comfort of those around me urges me on."[3] To assist her at home, Jane owned at least two slaves, perhaps more. (The 1850 census records her owning two; the 1860 personal property tax records indicate that four enslaved African-Americans lived on the Beale property.) Jane herself conveys her thoughts on the institution of slavery in her journal, stating that African-Americans, "were ordained of high Heaven to serve the white man and it is only in that capacity they can be happy useful and respected."[4]

Still, after the death of her husband, her toils included tasks unending. She recorded her activities for one late-summer day: "Spent part of the day greening pickles, cutting out work, cleaning lamps, learning lessons to the children, superintending the cleaning of the yards and whitewashing part of the house [,] pareing [sic] peaches, mending clothes, cleaning bedsteads of insects, seeing the cow milked & fed, nursing the baby, and after putting the children to bed sat down to knit and talk to Sam about my own and his plans for the winter."[5]

Interspersed with her writings on day-to-day activities, Jane's early entries also allude to episodes and events with importance that ascends to a national level. The slavery and States Rights controversy had just begun to preoccupy the American people in the summer of 1850 when she wrote her first entry, and her local worldview was directly impacted by political actions on the national theatre. She specifically observed two important events that are symbolic of the crisis soon to envelop the nation: the Compromise of 1850 and the passage through Fredericksburg of the body of Senator John C. Calhoun to his native South Carolina. Calhoun had been one of the most ardent defenders of States Rights and the institution of slavery.

When she again took up her pen and journal in 1861 after several years absence, Beale commenced recording the steady, tumultuous transformation of her world, town, and family by war: her sons off to fight; the deadly plague of scarlet fever that ravaged Fredericksburg's children in late 1861 and early 1862; the coming of the Yankees that spring, with all of its attendant annoyances and outrages; the steady adaptation to a life under occupation; the death of her son, Charley, at the Battle of Williamsburg; the physical explosion of war into her neighborhood and home on December 11, 1862, and her subsequent experience as a refugee; and the disruption of slavery that attended the presence of Union armies (her commentary on slavery is among the most valuable wartime testimonies on the gradual end of the practice in Fredericksburg).

A PLACE IN TIME

From the intensely personal to the profoundly important, Jane Beale's diary offers a rare and invaluable rendering of a tumultuous time, recorded by a mind and soul shaped by tragedy, challenged by imminent disaster, but bound to persevere. We have no picture of Jane Beale. But, we do have something far less common: a literary journey into her soul, giving us an unsurpassed look at both a woman and community in dramatic transition.

In this edition, the editors have kept their explanatory comments to a minimum. Her spelling and punctuation are reproduced as they appear in her own handwriting. The volume concludes with three poems, which appeared at the end of her journal. These poems were probably added at a later date to fill the remaining two pages in the journal, but they are a window into the mind of this brave, honest woman: "That care and trial seem at last / Through memory's sunset air / Like mountain ranges overpast / In purple distance fair." ▪

PART ONE

"Let Me Leave All Things To God's Disposal"

1850

AUGUST 27TH

This day my two eldest sons left me to accompany their Aunt Mrs. Sterling[6] to Prince Edward and remain perhaps two years. I am sad and lonely, but I take comfort in the belief that they will derive benefit from Mr. Sterlings instructions and acquire a certain degree of hardness which will better fit them for the combat of life, than if they had remained with a fond indulgent Mother. My Sisters have also gone and my cheerful niece, and I wander from room to room now laying my head down upon the spot where one week ago my beloved Mother[7] breathed her last breath, and wishing if I dared to sleep beside her, for I have no bosom friend to sympathise in my deep sorrow now. Alas! I have been a widow four months and sorrow has made deep inroads upon my mind since that dreadful day, but for an abiding trust in a "God Merciful Gracious Long-Suffering, Abundant in Goodness & Truth" I should indeed be a miserable creature but I have nine almost helpless children, am poor and

The Home of William and Jane Beale at 307 Lewis Street. Jane lived in the house from 1846 until her death in 1882.[8]

in a measure, dependant. Hourly exertion is called for on my part. I have the kindest most affectionate of brothers & Sisters, the best of friends, my health and that of my family is good, my children are lovely and intelligent my servants faithful and considerate. Verily Thou has not left me destitute even of temporal Good My Father in Heaven, and Thy chastising Rod better fits me for the performance of duty here, and for "that inheritance with the saints in light hereafter," I must bear it patiently and taking no merit to myself, but leaning on an All-sufficient Arm for my support, must go forward in this straight and narrow road, until that joyful summons comes, that happy hour arrives when I shall be called to join those I so dearly love in a brighter better world. In the after part of the day friends came in to cheer my solitude with conversation. 2 cousins from the country took tea and remained all night at my house I was glad to have them do so.

AUGUST 28TH

Rose early and looked out upon one of the loveliest mornings, that ever gladdened my eyes, dressed my children and read to them a portion of the Psalms, lifted my heart in prayer to the Giver of all Good that he would make them His children, and remembered those who had gone from me and earnestly prayed that the Arms of everlasting Mercy might be around them. After performing various active household duties sat down to my sewing work, with a more quiet and comfortable feeling than I had enjoyed for sometime, was interrupted by a visit from two old Christian friends of my Mother, who talked to me delightfully about her, one of them with a fine strong mind and more imagination than usually flourishes at the advanced age of 70 compared my Mother and her children as she had recently seen them, to a bunch of Cluster Roses one of which had decayed and was about to fall from the rest but was still sweet, while all the rest bloomed in freshness the other lady was the teacher of my Sisters and myself and a more generous heart never beat in human breast—I am confident, she promised to come tomorrow and dine with me.

I finished my work, and after my children had all retired to rest at night, my dear brother and myself sat reading by the lamp in my pleasant dining-room, something he read to me reminded me of the contents of a letter I had received some years since from my beloved Husband[9] and I went to the drawer where I had deposited all the letters I had ever received from him and brought them out and indulged myself by reading them again, this is the greatest earthly pleasure left to me now, but oh! the deep deep sorrow that follows its indulgence, can any affliction be compared to it, when I remember the devoted love he bore me evidenced in a thousand acts looks and words of kindness, and then the realizing sense, that I shall experience it no more, comes over me, I am crushed to the earth by sorrow, and am forced to seek consolation in prayer that my heart may be made submissive to the Will of God.

AUGUST 29TH

My old friend and teacher came early to spend a long and social day with me, she talked, of her residence in Charlottesville of Professor Davis's death, and the effect produced upon his family by the great change in circumstances which followed this sad event, these details, tho very sad, gave me hope and courage to hold on my onward course of exertion for my family, believing that all things will work together for good to those who trust the Lord.

My kind friend and neighbour Mrs. Bankhead came around this afternoon bringing with her a paper containing an Obituary of my Mother written by herself, but no eulogies of friends can add to my estimation of her worth, it is graven on my heart

Dr. Thomas and Virginia Knox House at 1201 Princess Anne Street.

by recollections of my early days which can never be effaced, another friend Mrs. Hays also came in and we had a pleasant chat, she was just from the bedside of my friend V. Knox[10] who has her 10th son, spend the evening until 10 o'clock reading newspapers and talking to my dear brother, who leaves a circle of gay and cheerful young friends, lest *I* should be lonely I cannot so poorly reward him as to indulge in melancholy reminescences constantly intruded upon him, I have talked of his affairs rather than my own, that I might be cheerful.

AUGUST 30TH

Rose late after being disturbed by my babe who seemed unwell in the night, and oppressed feeling was upon me as I remembered that this was the day for the execution of Prof. Webster,[11] but I felt truly thankful that with all my sorrows I was myself rather than that miserable wife, spent part of the morning in writing a letter to my dear Lucy Cooke[12] now on a visit to her Sister[13] in Albemarle, brother Jno[14] came in to dinner and we talked of business connected with the expected sale of property, I could not help expressing to him my earnest desire to continue to reside in the house where I have been so happy with my dearly loved husband, my wish to become the purchaser, provided it does not sell for more than my means will allow. We were interrupted in our conversation by Sam's[15] return from the Ft. with a gentleman from California who had recently been with our youngest brother and gave us agreeable information about him, Mr. Jenkins is a sensible plain young man, who brings no refinement with him from the distant land of gold, but it can scarcely be expected with reason that much refinement should exist where no Female Influence is felt and but little Religious influence. They took tea with me and then went to visit some young ladies, and after I had placed my children in bed, I sat down to read the 16th no. of David Copperfield, it contains a highly wrought picture of the misery which is produced by a sinful course of conduct, and made such an impression upon me that I was glad to escape from it, by falling asleep.

AUGUST 31ST

Saturday a busy day, preserving damsons for Sister Nannie,[16] mending and assorting childrens clothes, my eyes were blinded with tears as I opened the press doors and saw the empty shelves which had been appropriated to my dear Willie and Johnnie.[17] I am almost afraid of myself that I shall not be able to bear the long absence which may be necessary to complete their education, but I pray daily for wisdom from above to direct me in the right way and strength to pursue it, my kind Christian friends

Miss Kitty & Miss Ellen Lomax[18] called and by their cheerful Christian conversation did much to restore my spirits. I do love to see those ladies they seem to bring the refreshing atmosphere of Heaven into the House with them. In all the deep afflictions through which I have passed during the last 2 years they have been the first to come to my side, with words of consolation drawn from Holy Writ, with fervent prayers, and tender tears and have done all that friends could do to soothe my sorrows

The Home of Rebecca and Kitty Lomax at 1200 Princess Anne Street during the mid-nineteenth century. This dwelling is adjacent to the Beale House, and Jane recounted several visits to their home in her journal.

May God reward them for their goodness to me for I can never do it. My brother came in much earlier in the evening than usual and observing an unusual restlessness about him I enquired the cause, he told me that my Husband's eldest Son[19] (not mine thank Heaven) had been observed to leave the cars a few miles from this place and he feared he might under cover of night pay me a visit, as alas! his acts forbid his return to this place in the broad light of day this information created a state of uncomfortable expectation not amounting to fear, that he should come in and I should not be able to take that firm course towards him which would best tend to rid me of the annoyance of his presence perhaps of his troublesome demands upon me, he was the only great source of unhappiness which existed in our family during my married life and caused his father so much misery that it is hard for me to exercise a spirit of forgiveness towards him, and yet I think I could not turn away in hardness of heart even from him if I saw him in deep distress and showing signs of penitence.

SEPTEMBER 1ST

Enjoyed a pleasant reading of the Scriptures early this morning, part of it was a Chapter containing a rehearsal of the acts of the Almighty towards the children of Israel during their wanderings in the Wilderness in one of the verses it is said, "He gave them their *desires* but sent *leanness* into their souls" this seemed to have a new meaning to me and after reflecting upon it I felt that it was better to have the desires of our hearts taken away, rather than retain them at so heavy an expense. Went to church with my two little boys Charles and Robert, and listened to a most impressive and encouraging Sermon from our own beloved Pastor Mr. McPhail.[20] His text was that beautiful verse from the first Chapter of John "Behold the Lamb of God

The Presbyterian Church at the corner of Princess Anne and George Streets. The Beale family were members of the congregation during most of the nineteenth century. (*National Park Service*)

which taketh away the sin of the world" hurried home to escape a rain which soon fell in torrents, and spent the evening nursing the baby to allow the nurse to attend preaching, the babe slept a little giving me time to teach C & R a short lesson but so interrupted by the romps of two others who have not yet arrived at reasonable ages, that I fear they derived but little profit from it, the Sabbath is no day of rest to me now I have so many very young children I cannot teach the older ones with any pleasure and have no opportunity for reading and meditation, until night comes on and then alas! poor human nature I am so worn out with the fatigues of the day that I am too stupid to enjoy the one or engage in the other without falling asleep. I fear I am neither so energetic or so self-denying as my dear Mother was, for I have known her often to spend half the night reading after a day of constant exertion for the comfort of her family, this dear Mother was the very Sun of our domestic circle, we revolved around her like the Planets in our Solar System and shone by her reflected light, what a fountain of love filled her heart for her children, how it bubbled up and sent its pure refreshing streams over the pathway of our early life, my father[21] was not a man to bear with the faults & follies of childhood patiently, he had a numerous family, and a salary as a Bank Officer, scarcely sufficient to meet the constant demands upon him besides this he suffered at times from a very painful desease, and these causes combined made him morose and fretful, and we were often glad to escape from his presence and seek the tender, encourageing conversation of our dear Mama, we always found her at night seated at a little table in the dining-room strewed with books and a large basket of stockings to darn by her side, there have I sat beside her and told all my joys and all my sorrows into her interested and sympathizing ear, and received from her lips while her mind was in its strength the wisest counsel for the government of my conduct.

I have spun this day out very long but when I get in the midst of bye-gone years I know not when to quit the subject and feel inclined to go into a regular family history but as the members of our household were too numerous to give each one more than a passing glance I will reserve any farther notice of them until circumstances draw them to the light in the progress of each days journal.

SEPTEMBER 2ND

The morning was damp and cloudy causing one to feel painful and heavy, I have for some months past suffered with a painful oppression in my chest & side when I have been subjected to exposure, and I sometimes think that I have not yet entirely escaped from the effects of a severe attack of pleurisy I had last winter, or these may be warnings to prepare for my latter end, as most of my family have died with deseases of the heart, if so I must be quiet about it as I do not wish my dear children to feel any uneasiness about being left orphans in this world at an early period, but I must think the more, and endeavour to be prepared for this change, come when it will, My niece Mattie T.[22] came up and spent the day with me and was very pleasant and affectionate, she is a pretty sweet girl of 17 and every one who sees her seems attracted to her. My brothers Jno & Sam came to dinner at 3 and the latter remarked that this was his 25th birthday, whereupon we all drank a glass of wine to his health and future prosperity. Finished preserving my damsons and mended several articles of children's clothing.

SEPTEMBER 3RD

A day without incident, rose at 6 o'clock and went through my usual exercises without much spirit or interest, felt all day very indifferent towards the things of this world, without having a lively interest in that which lies beyond the tomb, I am often very stupid and dull now and wish I could feel more interest in what concerns me so much. Spent part of the day greening pickles, cutting out work, cleaning lamps, learning lessons to the children, superintending the cleaning of the yards and whitewashing part of the house pareing peaches, mending clothes, cleaning bedsteads of insects, seeing the cow milked & fed, nursing the baby, and after putting the children to bed sat down to knit and talk to Sam about my own and his plans for the winter, our attention was also directed to some beautiful Scripture prints which were my dear Mother's, and were taken from celebrated paintings of Westall's. These seem to have been very numerous and diversified employments for one so indifferent to every thing, but they are all necessary to the comfort of the numerous family by which I am surrounded and I must go through the Round even though my thoughts are far away. Oh that this state of dull despair of finding pleasure in earthly things, might have a tendency to reanimate my soul in pursuit of a happy home of eternal rest where my Saviour and his angels dwell.

SEPTEMBER 4TH

Overslept the time and rose to find the Sun shining brightly and far above the Chatham Hill, and felt a little conscience-stricken for my laziness as I had not been disturbed in the night and there was no excuse for me, the bad effect of course followed of having to hurry through every thing to get breakfast in proper time, but the children were quiet and good and I got my business in a regular train for the day by 9 o'clock, after performing my morning duties I paid a visit to Helen[23] whom I had found seated by the cradle, sewing and rocking little "Helen Roberta" at the same time, it was the first time I had seen her since the death of our beloved Mother and our hearts were full and would have overflowed in mingled sorrows for our own loss and joy in her eternal gain, but others, and those uninterested persons were by and we kept our feelings within our own bosoms, it was better perhaps as Helen looked pale and fatigued over the baby and she ought not to have given way to excited feeling. I found Sam there with 3 letters for which I received joyfully from his hands and immediately broke the seals, the first one I read was from Willie and as it was nearly his first effort in that line I was prepared for something like a failure, but to my glad surprise I found it a well expressed letter of two pages, with not more than 2 words spelled wrong, and none left out as is frequently the case with young writers I had a double pleasure in reading this letter as it contained information of their safe arrival at Hampden Sydney College, and of their good health, besides exhibiting a maturity of intellect which is rarely met with in a boy of 12 years of age, his observations

The Carmichael House at 309 Hanover Street. Jane was a close friend of Miss Ellen Carmichael who lived in this home with her parents, James and Elizabeth.

of men, and things were accurate and his descriptions graphic, and concise he said my poor little timid Johnnie was very much frightened at first upon going through the Locks on the Canal, but got accustomed to being lifted up and depressed by the water without being overwhelmed.

The next letter I opened was from my eldest daughter[24] and I always feel as if I were poring over the pages of some delightful author when reading her letters, so much good sense good taste sprightliness and fine feeling are to be found in her letters, that even a less partial judge a fond mother would be interested in their contents, my third letter was from my niece Helen Winder who left me last week and contained nothing but pleasant news from our friends in Norfolk, with an amusing account of their trip down. I returned home at 2 o'clock and, we had beefsteak, and then apple-dumpling at 3, and then sat down to my sewing, had a visit from 2 little Miss Bankheads who came to read the children's letters if I had no objection, I had not the least, far from it I felt grateful for the interest manifested in those so dear to me, by others and cheerfully gave them the letters to read, they are very intelligent children and their conversation really entertained me, after they left, dressed my sweet pretty little babe and sent him to see Miss Ellen Carmichael[25] by her own request, I am a very proud Mother, but I hope I may not forget the important truth that I am but a Steward for my Lord and must one day yield my account to him of my management of these as well as other trusts He has confided to me for a time.

SEPTEMBER 5TH

Early in the morning, cleared the dining room and Chamber for a Man to Whitewash the Ceilings and of course every thing was thrown into confusion for several hours I sat down in the parlour to write letters and amidst much confusion & interruption got through 2, one to my dear Son Willie which I have no doubt will give him exquisite pleasure as it is the first letter he has ever received directed to himself and the other to Helen Winder, these with the various employments incident to every day filled up the hours until 9 PM when feeling wearied and having no company I retired. Sam went up with brother Jno to stay all night.

SEPTEMBER 6TH

Spent the whole morning writing to my dear brother Ned who is now a resident of Stockton Upper California, he is the youngest of our numerous family has a remarkably intelligent mind and in my eyes a very handsome person, is just 22 years of age and has already made for himself a Character. He lived with us for several years, and when the Gold excitement broke out in Cal 2 years ago, became very anxious to try his fortune in that distant land he was enabled to carry this design into execution by the assisstance of my dear Husband, and left us 18 months ago, to cross the Isthmus and take his way to San Francisco and the Mines in Cal, he did long continue in the Mining business but joined another brother[26] who was engaged in a profitable business in the town of Stockton and is now reaping the reward of his resolution and perseverance in the accumulation of a handsome property. He manifested some preference for a talented young lady in this neighbourhood before he left and may return one of these days, drawn by the strong attraction of early attachment, as well as by the cords of family affection which bind us more closely together than most families.

Had visits from some of my neighbours in the evening, one of whom remained until after tea.

SEPTEMBER 7TH

Rain poured down all the morning and kept us within doors, a noisy party the children were, and so I shut them up in a room to themselves, and sat down in the parlour to finish my letter to Ned, I had made not much progress, when a carriage drove to the door and I had the happiness of seeing my dear brother James's face at the window, my mind was greatly relieved by this arrival as he remained so much longer than I expected that I feared he was ill somewhere in the mountains, he told me that he had been with a pleasant party from Baltimore, rambling from one Watering Place to another and visiting all the curiosities of that Mountainous region, he is an unmarried gentleman of 30 years and is the Aristocrate of the family, tho it is a very noble kind of Aristocracy which possesses his mind, not that which elevates mere wealth with its appurtenances into an object of adoration but a love of refinement, polish and true beauty of character and manners in those he selects for his associates, and an abhorrence of every thing mean, vulgar and pretending, we sat for an hour talking over scenes which preceded the death of our much beloved deeply revered mother, and his heart was full of sorrow at the thought of not being here to receive her parting benediction. Brothers Jno & Sam drove up soon after, in a handsome buggy just purchased by the latter, and in which the former was about to take a trip to Fauquier. The Northern Mail brought delightful long letters from my dear Ned in which he expresses so much affectionate sympathy for me as to touch my very heart, surely no one ever had cause to be more grateful to Divine Providence than I, for all the blessings he has showered upon my path.

St. George's Episcopal Church on Princess Anne Street.

SUNDAY SEPTEMBER 8TH

Our own pastor being absent on a visit to his aged and declining father, my brothers and myself attended the Episcopal Church and heard a plain sensible discourse from the Rev. Mr. McGuire.[27] This gentleman has long been a resident of our town and bears a strong resemblance to my dear old father, so that this is sufficient to make me love to see him and hear him. Spent the evening chiefly in conversation with my brothers, and deferred the children's lessons until night when they were gotten through with more pleasure than usual.

The Home of Reverend Edward McGuire, rector of St. George's Church and Beale family friend, at 1100 Charles Street.

MONDAY SEPTEMBER 9TH

Another rainy day, which was devoted chiefly to paring and cutting peaches to preserve, wondered while I was engaged in this way whether it was worth the time spent, to enjoy the advantage of possessing them, arrived at the specious conclusion that I would not do it for myself but that I was working for the comfort and benefit of others, brother John arrived from Fauquier to tea, wet & weary and I was busy for a time making him comfortable, and after tea my 3 brothers and myself sat down to a pleasant family chat.

SEPTEMBER 12TH

Have neglected my diary for a few days owing to a great variety and number of domestic employments during the day and company to a late hour every evening, I think sometimes I am very like "Martha" of "Bethany" "careful and troubled about many things" but I have the excuse that *all* the business of a large family has suddenly devolved upon me, that I have not been fitted by early education for later habits, for this employment, that my mind is not constituted to love it, and it is therefore a toil and drudgery to me which it would not otherwise be, I seem to be doing something I do not like all the time, but a strong sense of duty combined with an earnest desire to secure the comfort of those around me urges me on.

This season of the year brings with it not only its own employments for every day but a vast number in preparation for the inclement season that follows it, and if we do not work ourselves and make others do the same, we will find ourselves in the midst of winter soon, and by no means comfortable. My brothers are still with me and add more that I can express to the pleasure of my family circle, Brother John is now the oldest Son of the family and his locks are beginning to look a little frosty about the temples, tho his brow is still unfurrowed, he is an officer in the Va. Bank and resides on a pretty little farm near town, where he enjoys in his family as much happiness as ever falls to the lot of mortals in this world, he is the Administrator of the Estate left by my husband and is my aid and counsellor in every thing. His heart is full of the most genuine benevolence, and his thoughts pure and upright, tho he has a plain manner of expressing himself that sometimes gives offense to those who do not know him perfectly, there are a great many grown up children in the world who require humouring, and cannot bear to be told the truth, and when our dear brother comes in contact with those, he is often terribly at fault, for want of a little of the oil of flattery upon his tongue. But he gains daily upon the confidence and respect of those who know him best. To day James joined a party of friends who came on from the Springs and accompanied them to the Steam Boat Landing, I am rather inclined to suspect him of having a penchant for a fair lady of that party, a niece of Mrs. Jerome Buenoparte [Bonaparte]. I shall watch him, he did not get back to dinner and I hear some accident occurred to detain the cars, brother Jno Sam and I dined together and after dinner Sam sent for his buggy and we took a delightful long ride, it has been so long since I enjoyed this pleasure, that I felt some exhilleration of spirits as we whirled rapidly along through the smooth lanes, and I inhaled the odour of field and forest borne upon the cool Fall atmosphere. Sam talked a good deal of Nannie and

I will here digress to introduce this pair, to whom? Why to themselves if they should perchance get hold of these pages in after years, it will perhaps amuse them to find themselves showed up as they appear now, Sam is the brother to whom I alluded as having been engaged in a profitable business in Stockton UC. He returned to his home and friends in Va. last May after having been absent more than 3 years. His return was the occassion of deep joy and gratitude to me as it occurred just 1 month after the death of my dear Husband, when our affairs looked dark and unpromising and besides the agony of grief which I suffered on account of his loss, I could not see the means by which my children were to be maintained.

Sam's return with means and will to aid me was the first encouraging circumstance which brightened the dark horizon by which I had been surrounded for many week, He determined at once to abandon all thoughts of returning to Cal, and putting one half his money out at interest, to engage with the rest in some business which would employ his time agreeably and profitably. He is just 25 years of age is handsome gay and agreeable, and these qualities very soon won for him the affections of one of the lovliest daughters of Va. Miss Nannie F—[28] who has not very long been a resident of Fred'g, was born and raised near Winchester, she is about 17 years of age, of middle height and somewhat slender form, has perfect features, a rose like bloom upon her cheek, which with a large mild steel-grey eye renders her a star of the first magnitude in beauty. Of her character and manners I know but little as I have rarely met with her, but I am destined to become well-acquainted ere long as they will be married in Nov. and are then to live with me.

SEPTEMBER 13TH

James returned to-day after accompanying Miss P— all the way to Wash. which circumstance tended to confirm my suspicions tho' he avows innocence. Nous verrons! as old Mr. Ritchie says, the mention of this gents name reminds me that Congress has this week passed several important Bills the discussion of which has agitated both Houses for many months, the admission of California as a State, the Texas and New Mexico Bill, and the Fugitive Slave Bill, we may now hope that peace will be restored to our agitated Country tho' there are probably many both North and South who are not satisfied with the Passage of the Bills, I hope their ultraism will not affect the general quiet. Our Papers from the North are now filled with the Debut of Jenny Lind, which took place at Castle Garden, New York where she sung to an audience of 25,000 and filled them with rapturous admiration her part of the proceeds of this concert amounted to $10,000 which she distributed among the Established Charities of the City. How happy she must be to have it in her power to delight one portion of mankind with her vocal powers, and to open her hand wide in bestowing blessings upon another portion.

SEPTEMBER 14TH

Rose with a headache after being much disturbed during the night by my little Minnie who had a fever and was evidently quite sick administered a dose of medicine which I hope may be all that will be necessary for her restoration, after breakfast filled corked and sealed my Catsup bottles, tied up & marked Pickle and Preserve pots, wrote up my Daily account Book, mended and assorted my children's clothes, a letter came in the Southern Mail from Sister Ann, my eldest Sister resident in Norfolk she is the beauty of the family, or perhaps I should say 'has been' as she is now past 40 and of course is not quite so fresh and blooming as she was, she has however a kind of beauty which will never fade a fine intellectual grey eye with a set of Chiselled features, the beautiful proportions of which, age only serves to develope more perfectly. She has been married twice, first to James D. Thorburn Merchant of Norfolk, and last to Capt. Thos. Dornin of the Navy, her family consists of 3 grown children (Thorburn's) the 2 daughters married to naval officers and at present with her, and the Son a Midship'n in the Navy, altogether a complete Naval concern, there are also 4 little Dornin's ranging from 12 years to 4. After getting through the business of the day, sat down to a game of Chess with Sam and was soon Check-mated gave up my place to James and went upstairs to put the children to bed, and get out all their clean clothes for Sunday morning.

SEPTEMBER 15TH

Rose early and had time to read an hour with pleasure before it was time to dress the children for breakfast, took two of them to church with me, where we listened with pleasurable interest to a Sermon from Mr Phail's text from the Psalms of David "Thou shalt guide me by thy counsel and afterwards receive me into glory" I was filled with an earnest desire to be guided by the Counsel's of unerring Wisdom through the bustle and tumult of life, and Oh how ardently I longed for rest among the glorified in Heaven. Our pastor looked pale and dejected he has just returned from a visit to his parents who have been afflicted by the death of a Son older than himself. As usual nursed, during the afternoon, and had the privilege of attending Church with my brothers again in the evening, but was not so much interested as I was in the morning owing to my own stupidity I have no doubt, the text was again from the Psalms 63d c 8th v, "My soul followeth hard after God."

THURSDAY, SEPTEMBER 19TH

Nothing has occurred to interest me much during the last 3 days, I have been engaged writing letters, altering dresses, getting repairs made and the house put in order for cold weather. I had one pleasant ride around by Falmouth and the sight of those familiar scenes roused up many a dormant memory of the past, for it was there, yes in that brick house on the bank of the river so shaded by trees, that I went as a happy bride to take up my abode 16 years ago, and despite of the peculiar trials which always attend

Located across the Rappahannock River in Falmouth, newlyweds William and Jane Beale lived in this home until moving into town in 1846. It was later the home of noted abolitionist Moncure Daniel Conway.

the lot of a stepmother, it was there I spent 5 years as happily as ever woman did upon this earth, for I was united to one whom my heart preferred to any one I had ever seen or heard of he was indeed worthy of all the affection that could have been bestowed upon him, of a noble gentlemanly character a refined and cultivated mind, the mildest lovliest temper and disposition that ever dwelt in human breast. Who would not have loved him almost to adoration? When I remember that I have been the loved and honoured wife of such a man, my heart revolts at the idea of ever, in thought, word or deed descending from the proud station which I occupied in my own view, and in his opinion and I can never forget that his name, his honor is involved with mine in all that I do or say. I have 6 sons, and I can only hope they may all resemble him, they are left without fortune, but his name is a glorious inheritance to them, and if they will only follow in his footsteps they need nothing but the blessing of Almighty God to make them good, prosperous and happy. I had a visit yesterday from an old schoolmate and our conversation turned upon early days, after she left I spent some time looking over old letters in order to burn up the chaff amongst them, and I felt as if I had gone back some 20 years and was living over again amongst those home scenes so graphically described by the excellent letter writers in our family, my father excelled in the art I think, and wrote in such handsome legible characters that it is a pleasure to read his letters, I believe I have spoken of him before as a man of impatient temper, but with this he had a most affectionate heart and a sound understanding, and guided his children in paths of truth and honour, we cannot be sufficiently grateful to our dear kind parents for the care they took of us in childhood and the example they have left us.

SEPTEMBER 21ST

Yesterday my dear Sam left me to bring my daughters back from Albemarle where they have been spending the summer with a half-Sister, I look forward with pleasure to their return, for tho' I have 5 small children with me, I miss the society of my older children, losing the companionship of my beloved husband and my dear Mother so suddenly and with so short an interval between, makes me feel truly an "aching void" a constant craving want. Oh that the throne of my heart might be filled by the presence the manifested presence of my Savior, I wish not to feel that I have been hardly dealt by, that I have an "austere Master" reaping where he has now sown, no let me bow down submissively before Him saying "It is the Lord let Him do what seemeth good in his sight" let me feel that "he doth not needlessly afflict."

I received a letter to-day from my Son Willie with a postscript from dear little Johnnie so truly characteristic of him that I scarcely know whether to laugh or cry over it, they are a little home-sick but I hope they will soon get over it and make themselves as happy as they can, they have commenced studying with much earnestness, I pray that they may grow up to be good and useful men and that the world may be benefitted by their having lived in it, tho' I have no ambitions thoughts or wishes that their influence shall be extended over a very wide circle. I had a visit from a lady requesting me to take her daughter as a boarder, which I consented to do, I hope she may be good, I want no unfavourable influences to operate upon my children, we must try and let none be brought to bear upon her young mind. I went this evening to see my next eldest Sister, "Helen" whom I have spoken of, she is so lovely and excellent as to deserve more than a passing notice, her appearance is extremely interesting and her character has been tried in a school of some severity, and thereby purified in an uncommon degree, and she is altogether one more fitted to be loved than any one else I know. She is also the Wife of a Naval Officer and has a family of 6 children, the eldest of whom is the sweet girl "Mattie" whom I have before spoken of.

SUNDAY, SEPTEMBER 22ND

Went to church with my children and listened to a very interesting sermon, from the text "Oh send out thy light to thy truth" felt very badly all day from a severe cold I have contracted, and did not go out at night in consequence, was much depressed in spirits all day, thoughts of by-gone days and by-gone happiness filled my mind and when my children had retired and I was left alone, gave myself up to excessive grief and grew so feeble in consequence that it became a task to undress and prepare for the night but I found some consolation in spreading my sorrows before a throne of grace and reminding our Compassionate Reedeemer that he had wept over the grave of Lazarous when upon earth. Oh that my sinful heart could give up its too earnest desires for earthly happiness, and wait for that which shall be revealed hereafter.

MONDAY, SEPTEMBER 23RD

Still felt deep depression, and feared sometimes I was left alone to bear my sorrows. Feel a certain conviction that it was the all-sustaining hand of Divine Providence which supported me at first, what else could have kept me from sinking weak as I then was with an infant only a few days old. Oh Memory I know not whether thou art a blessing or the reverse. Thou canst bring up so many "green spots" and refreshing fountains to mock me in this desert this dreary waste, and yet there is a pleasure in dwelling upon the past, which nothing in the future can give me, for my heart's idol dwells now only in one of memory's cells, he cannot go with me into the untried future, he cannot protect me from any dangers, soothe me under any troubles I may have to encounter therin, it is therefore the part of Wisdom to seek the assistance of One who can and "to whom else can I go but unto Thee O Lord, for Thou hast the words of Eternal Life."

I was glad to see dear brother John and his family drive up about dusk this evening for I am very lonely, and but for constant and active employment I should spend many miserable hours. I have found myself sometimes of late pitying from my very heart A Widow who was left without children and in affluence for what has she to take her thoughts off her own personal loss. I suppose however such an one would not readily change places with me. I am glad to derive some benefit from what would appear to be cause of great affliction.

SEPTEMBER 24TH

Spent a busy day, getting carpets down and arrangements made for cool weather, had a visit from brother Edward Beale,[29] and one from a Mr. Nax[30] the Music Teacher urging me to let him teach my Lucy, which I agreed to. A sense of obligation is painful to me and would be doubly so to her and so I told Mr. Nax that I would accept his kind offer and only oblige him to wait a little while for remuneration, as I hope to be able to discharge all my obligations in the course of the next year if Providence blesses me so far.

I had an application to take another boarder but felt unwilling to receive a perfect stranger into my family. In the afternoon, walked down the street with my little Minnie, visited my Sister, looked at some furniture for Sam, paid a short visit to the Dentist, and called on my return home a few moments at the house of a friend who is upon a bed of suffering herself, and her children have the whooping cough, tried to speak a few words of comfort to her, but felt my own sorrows pressing so heavily upon me, that the sight of hers only made one weep and I fear my visit only depressed her the more.

SEPTEMBER 25TH

Rose early and enjoyed the cool morning air, after a walk around the garden, took the Bible and read the beautiful argument of the Apostle Paul for Justification by faith contained in the 4th, 5th & 6th of Romans. Soon after breakfast, was called to the parlour to see a gentleman, and found my Husband's eldest brother, Mr. John Beale, I feel quite near enough to him to call him 'brother' but he appears so much older than I, that I scarcely know how to give him that title. How my heart warms to all *his* brothers, how grateful I feel for the interest they show in me and my children, I promised to pay a visit to Fauquier where he resides and take *all* my little ones. I hope he may not have cause to regret his kindness in giving me the invitation.

SEPTEMBER 26TH

Paid another visit to the Dentist this morning and had 3 teeth filled, one of which gave me considerable pain. Received the *agreeable* information from Dr. Lawrence that it was necessary that 4 of my teeth should be extracted.[31] I fear I shall never make up my mind to undergo the operation. I believe I am more than usually weak and selfish as it regards bodily pain, for even when I know what it will procure subsequent comfort and tend much to my future usefulness, I shrink from it like an animal of mere instinct, instead of one guided by thought and reason.

SEPTEMBER 27TH

This is my little Edward Julian's birth day, and brings with it many tender associations. I have had him a cake made and the other children offer their congratulations in rather a rough manner. The little fellow stands in their midst wondering what it all means, but evidently knowing that it has some reference to himself, and showing the common dispostion to self-exaltation in the manner he struts up and down the

Many members of the Howison and Beale families are interred at the Fredericksburg City Cemetery. From left to right are the graves of William Churchill Beale (Jane's husband), Jane Howison Beale, John Howison Beale (William and Jane's fourth child), and Charles Dornin Beale (William and Jane's fifth child who died in battle during the Civil War).

pavement. Spent the morning sewing, and walked up in the afternoon to brother John's to see Sister Nanny, we got some fine garden grapes and the little boys enjoyed their visit very much, on our return, we found the gate of the Cemetery open and went in, it was the first time I had been there since my beloved husband and my mother were interred and the grass was green above the resting place of him I still sorrow for, how still and sad it seemed, no kind voice issued from that narrow cell to bid me be of good cheer and walk firmly and courageously forward in the path of duty, and I felt truly alone in the world, with tremendous interest involved in my course, my heart seemed almost bursting with grief and I tore myself away from the spot, lest I should indulge the selfish the wrong desire, to lay my weary head and aching heart down in the peaceful grave with my own much love—

SEPTEMBER 28TH

My dear daughters arrived in the Cars to-day from Albermarle accompanied by my brother Sam, how glad I was to see them looking so fresh and healthy, their return has quite roused me up from the lethergy of sadness into which I had sunk, I shall try and be more cheerful for their sakes as well as my own.

Had a visit this afternoon from Mrs. J. L. Marye[32] a very pleasant kind-hearted lady, her son and daughter came with her to see my girls.

SATURDAY, OCTOBER 5TH

A week has passed since I made an entry in my Diary, during which time, constant employment during the day and company at night have prevented me from writing, I have got all my Carpets down, all my Pickles made, made all necessary purchases for fitting up my brother's room, but have been chiefly engaged nursing my Lucy who has suffered much from disordered stomach and depression of spirits, it has disstressed me much to observe that the fear of an early death should check the exhuberance of her youthful spirits and throw a gloom over her prospects. May God grant that this fear may lead to sincere contrition of heart for sins and a trust in a Crucified Redeemer, for the sooner she "turns away her thoughts from beholding vanity" the better for her happiness in this world as well as that which is to come.

My eldest daughter has commenced her studies with an energy which promises success in the acquisition of knowledge and as I watch the operations of her superior mind, I feel that her carreer in life will be a useful one, tho' she may never be distinguished by the world's applause. Oh that she too may be guided by the Spirit of God, an learn in "all her ways to acknowledge Him." The world with all its interests seems to occupy a smaller space, and to be of far less value than it formerly appeared, and sometimes in conversation with my children I check myself to suit their present youthful views of things as I am sensible that they must learn the worthlessness of all earthly things in procuring true happiness from their own experience and not from mine, and I want them to be happy and cheerful.

OCTOBER 9TH

Have received several delightful affectionate letters during the past week, from my step-daughter in Albemarle, my sister in Norfolk and my dear brother in California. His letter was addressed to our beloved Mother and her familiar name upon the face of it, filled me with sadness, he has just about this time received news of her death, and no doubt feels it deeply. I wish I was near him to tell him many things which would tend to reconcile and especially to point him to that Star of Bethlehem which guided her through the dark pilgrimage of this world, and rose bright over her dying pillow.

OCTOBER 18TH

Another week has passed and I have to record, only mercies, blessings far above our deserts. In the first place the health of the family continues good even through this trying season of the year, and tho' I have suffered some anxiety on account of the little girl who boards with me that has been removed by her recovery from what I feared would have been a dangerous and protracted spell of illness. My dear Lucy is also better and more cheerful and when the family party assembles around the bright Lamp-light in the evening, with their joyous merry tumult of voices, I feel that I can almost sympathise in their happiness that I am still sensible that the happiness is *not mine,* but only anothers that I can in some measure help them to enjoy, I am oppressed with a constant sense of lonliness even when surrounded with my family and I forget this utter desolation, except when I can cast myself upon the All-sustaining Arm which rules and guides the Universe. I have received letters from my absent Sons and my Sisters also and have heard no bad news. I have had many *little kindnesses* shown me in friendly acts, and even the manners of all towards me are tender and gentle. I feel more now as if I belonged to *every body* than I formerly did and my heart goes out towards all my friends in pursuit of a small portion of that love, which was once treasured up so largely in *one* bosom for me, how can any human being bear with life who knows they are not loved. I had a visit last night from our pastor, he came and sat the evening with us and was so pleasant and kind that I was sorry when the hour came for him to leave. He gives my daughters great praise for their diligence in study and sweet deportment to all around them in school, and it delighted me to hear that they had his entire approbation, I hope they may ever exert themselves to deserve it.

I have been busily engaged nearly all day arranging our Library, and came to the conclusion that there was valuable reading enough in the house to last 50 years without buying any more books, my husband loved to read, works of old authors, the quaint sententious style of Hume suited his taste better than the more ornamented and prolonged sentences of McCauley, and tho' he read the History of England by the latter with interest, he would often draw comparisons in favour of Hume as a Historian. He would often allude to Dean Swift's writings, to Dr. Johnson, Addison and others of an old date, and said that many thoughts and sentiments, were original with them which have since been adopted and used by later authors as their own property, but were merely dressed up in a finer garb to prevent the plaguarism from being discovered.

Jane's brother John Howison and his family lived at this home at 1203 William Street, known as "Rose Hill." The dwelling was the center of a large farm on what was then the outskirts of town. The turrets and ironwork were added after the family sold the farm.

OCTOBER 24TH

I find now I must write when I have time or opportunity favours as I am so surrounded in the evening I can seldom write up the events of the day, and indeed the employments of the day tho' numerous are quite monotonous. I have been quite disturbed since I last wrote by learning of the failure of a gentleman in California who owed my brother $5,000, my interests are so much involved in the prosperity of this brother that I feel for myself as well as for him in this loss, but I give my children up to God daily and I am satisfied that "He who feeds the Ravens" will not allow "those who trust Him to want any good thing" I walked up to brother John's[33] yesterday evening, and found all our pleasant retired pathway, ploughed up and many workmen busy levelling the track for the Plank Roads.[34] I sighed to lose the quiet, grassy walk but confess it was a selfish perhaps illiberal sorrow for if this improvement is to benefit the community I should rather rejoice in it, but I feel so much like an isolated being now, having no part or lot in any of these things, that I could not help weeping to think that the only thing which concerned me was the *Cemetery,* and *that* was no longer to occupy the retired position which would enable me to seek it when I pleased, and not be exposed to the gaze of the indifferent, the vulgar, or the curious.

NOVEMBER 1ST

Called yesterday to see my *Sister that is to be,* found her looking fresh & lovely as a new blown rose, with pleasing unaffected manners, she was surrounded by a very pleasant circle of friends, her mother bears the stamp of meekness and resignation under sorrow, and trouble upon her pale face, and I feel a sympathy with her, for she was left a widow with a family of young children around her, tho I believe not quite so poor as I am. There were two young ladies also present, whose lovely blooming faces did not indicate that sorrow had pressed heavily on their young hearts, and yet they are pennyless orphans and teach school for their own support. I love to see that lofty independance of character in woman which teaches her to rely upon herself in trying exigencies, particularly when it is accompanied by a refind sensibility such as they exhibit. On our way home I encountered a gentleman to whom I owe a large debt of gratitude, he has just returned from a trip to Europe, and was surrounded by a circle of friends to whom he was relating some of the incidents of his voyage. I would gladly have told him how much I rejoiced in his restoration to his family and friends, how deeply grateful I felt, for his kindness to me, manifested just before his departure, but this was no time or place for the exhibition of feeling. I passed him with a swelling heart and eyes overflowing with tears, and could only pray that God would bless him with a treasure in Heaven far above that which he had bestowed upon him here. I had my dear little babe babtized this afternoon, and my Sister also brought her little Helen Roberta up. I think I never before felt so truly the import of this ceremony. I gave my baby up with *a freedom,* a *fearlessness* into the hands of God to do *just* what *He* would with him which I never experienced before, and the only reservation in my heart was, that this little one should not be *lost,* should not be suffered to walk the broad road which leads down to Eternal Death but that the Savior should early gather him into His fold, whether in Heaven or upon Earth seemed a matter of small concern with me.

NOVEMBER 7TH

The sermon on Sabbath Morning was a very interesting one the subject, the destruction of the world by the Flood. I find I have made a mistake it was the Sabbath previous my memory reverted to, the subject of the last Sabbath Morning was the necessity of preparation for Coming to the Sacrament of our Lord which is to be administered next Sunday Morning, and the text was the words used by one of the disciples to another in anticipation of the probable coming of the Savior to the Passover, "Think you that He will be there" it was a sermon well calculated to impress the minds of the people of God with an earnest desire to have His presence in His Ordinances. We attended the Prayer Meeting for Missions at night.

The 5th of this month was my eldest daughter's birthday, she has reached the age of 15, that happy period when all the scene looks bright and the world seems full of gladness, she is of a quiet turn of mind not easily excited, and makes very few outward demonstrations of her feelings whether pleasurable or sad, she appears less dependant upon others for her happiness than any young person I ever saw, and shut her up in a room by herself and you need only fill her little table with books and she is perfectly content, I should like to see her take more interest in things around her as I think she is too dreamy and imaginative now to be useful, and we must not live for ourselves in this world.

I received by the mail of the 6th a letter from my dear brother-in-law, Mr. Sterling, announcing the birth of a little girl, I was glad to hear of this, as they have had but one daughter before which they lost suddenly when she was 2 years of age, and whose death caused such intense grief to my Sister that her health was seriously impaired for months. She is my Youngest Sister and we were raised so much together that there has always been a peculiar tie between us, she is a person of the strongest affections, and her excellent sense and humourous disposition make her a most charming companion as well as a most valuable friend, they are residents of Prince Edward County as Mr. Sterling was elected Professor of Chemistry in the College of Hampden Sydney 2 years ago, I have placed my 2 eldest Sons under his care, for the benefit of his personal instructions, I have the highest opinon of his piety of his Capacity to impart knowledge and discipline the characters of those under his charge, and have been very glad to be able to give my boys up to him at this important period of their lives, for I have so many younger ones that require my personal attention that I should be compelled to neglect my older children, or leave them too much to their own guidance.

NOVEMBER 17TH

This has been a week of hurry and excitement. My brother[35] S was married on Thursday evening, and brought his lovely bride to dine with me yesterday. I did not attend the wedding for my heart was not attuned to gaity, and I did not wish to impair the enjoyment of others by presenting my sad face and deep mourning dress to view. I was however busily engaged assissting the girls in their preparations, making Sam's chamber nice & comfortable all the early part of the week, and getting ready to entertain the bridal party here the latter part. My daughters were dressed in white and while the elder one wore her usual sweet quiet look, Lucy, the second one, had her head dressed in new style exposing the whole beautiful contour of her face and was so lovely that I could not look upon her without the thought constantly intruding, "with what tender admiration her dear father would have regarded her had he been here tonight." Lucy was always a darling child of his and her disposition was perhaps a little injured by his too tender indulgence, it did not manifest itself while we were in affluence during his life but I fear she does not bear the privations to which we are now subjected with the same contented submission that her Sister does, and I watch the development of her character with some anxiety, I pray that our Heavenly Father may make our present circumstances useful to her young mind restraining vanity and excessive love of the world, which might otherwise have ensnared her.

The party yesterday amounted to 30 and was attended with all the bustle and confusion incident to such an occassion. I was glad of it for I did not want a moment to let memory act yesterday, I was fearful of myself all day and *talked* more than I felt inclined to do lest I should *think.* The bride was very beautiful young and modest, but I am not yet acquainted with her as our intercourse has been of an artificial character as yet. My brother seems very happy, long may his happiness continue.

MONDAY, NOVEMBER 18TH

Busy all day putting every thing in place after the dinner party Saturday. Had a visit from Sam and his bride in the afternoon and improved my acquaintance with her a little. This season of the year recalls many a tender association, the first letter I ever received from my beloved husband was dated this day 17 years ago, and what a new era of joy & happiness it opened to me, but I cannot trust myself on this subject I should write half a volume.

NOVEMBER 19TH

Employed all day assissting brother John's wife to get ready for an evening party to be given to the bridal pair, heard it went off very well.

NOVEMBER 20TH

A cloudy morning succeeded by a rainy day. Mama's house was offered for sale to-day, brother John would not let it go at less price than he valued it, and had to buy it. Sam & Nanny came up in a hack to take up their abode with me. I felt for her, leaving her

Jane's childhood home at 1300 Charles Street, now known as the "St. James House."

tender Mother's side to go among perfect strangers and she so young and unused to the world, and the necessity for exertion in her behalf has taken me out of myself and has perhaps been beneficial to me, I have had to help her to entertain her company and Oh I have worn many a smile upon my face when my heart was sad. Shall I ever have joy in my heart again? Not such as I have had I am *sure,* and how hard it is to give it up. As winter approaches my sadness is increased, for in that season we seemed to draw nearer together than ever and for a number of years my health has not admitted much out-door exercise during inclement weather and I have been almost dependant on my dear husband for company and for comfort, how can I spend the dark lonely hours of this winter without the cheering influence of his presence in the house. Oh my soul, gather up all thy powers and more earnestly than ever seek "that glorious inheritance that fadeth not away" for thou hast nothing here now.

DECEMBER 2

My little Sister Nannie has made an agreeable addition to our family circle and conributes very much to make home more cheerful and pleasant to my daughters, but poor Lucy has again been suffering with an attack of sickness accompanied by depressions and caused me more anxiety.

Attended Church twice on Sunday and heard two excellent sermons. Felt some concern to learn that my dear Sister Helen and her family were going away for 2 years as her husband has lately been promoted to be a Capt, and is ordered to take command of the Pensacola Navy Yard.

DECEMBER 4TH

Since I made the last entry in my journal I have had my heart pained by another cause, I have received letters from my dear Sister in Prince Edward mentioning the resignation of Mr. Sterling on account of injurious reports having been circulated respecting his capacity as a Professor.[36] He has 5 young children, is involved in debt and has no means of support but this, could any thing more deeply wound than this? With the loss of his reputation he loses everything, even his children's bread, is dependant upon this. Can he stand under this terrible blast which is now blowing over him, he is a true Christian gentleman, with intellectual capacities equal to any who wear those flimsey honours and moral qualities far superior to most of them. Our Father in Heaven will guide and direct this storm and bring his trusting servants safely through it, tho' now they seem in imminent danger of being wrecked.

I have written for my boys, and my dear brother Robert[37] has forwarded money to bring them home, this brother is the only one I have not had occassion to mention in my journal before, and he is the most distinguished member of the family too for he is an author of no mean merit, having written a history of Virginia which has been complimented by learned men and witty critics both in our own State and others, his has been rather an eventful life tho' he is still young. He has been Merchant Lawyer Minister, & Lawyer again, all by the force of circumstances rather than by any fickleness in his own disposition, he married a daughter of Dr. Graham of Prince Edward, and they live in the city of Richmond where he is rising rapidly in the estimation of the Community on account of his talents, his amiable agreeable deportment and the great punctuality and exactness in attention to business, which he shews.

If any eyes but mine should ever glance upon these pages they would judge ours to a family of perfection, but tho' I know that each member has his own faults they are but little perceptible to me and I choose only to dwell upon their virtues.

DECEMBER 5TH

This has been a week of rain and clouds, we have seen no ray of sunshine since Sunday last but the weather has but little effect upon me. My work is all indoors and requires such incessant exertion that I scarcely notice what goes on without. I have received a letter from my Son Willie with a sad postscript from my dear Sister, how this painful affair is to end is still uncertain. One thing I certainly know that I must give up the darling project I have entertained of having my boys educated by Mr. Sterling and how they are to be educated at all I cannot now see, but I trust the Lord will open to my view some means by which this desirable end can be accomplished, I can teach them many branches myself, but I should fail in others which are of much importance to them now and I had so long expected to give them really good educations, that it is the sorest Reflection which accompanies my reduced circumstances, that they must receive very slight advantages from schools.

DECEMBER 17TH

I have just parted with dear Helen and her little family, they have gone in the Baltimore boat this morning to that city to join the ship Charles bound for New Orleans from whence they will be conveyed in a Steam boat to their point of destination Pensacola Navy Yard. I tried to give her all the assisstance I could in nursing the baby and making the little boys neat before they started, took a hurried leave of my dear

Sister for I did not want her feelings to be excited at that anxious moment, but as I stood in the twilight of the gloomy deserted house after they had all gone, sad memories rushed over me and dark forbodings would not be shut out and I wept in bitterness of spirit, as each earthly comfort seemed passing away from me. Henceforth this world is to be but a sorrowful pilgrimage to me.

I went down this morning and saw that Helen's carpets were carefully packed away and every thing they left stowed in places of safety, and afterwards walked onto some of the stores at one of which I encountered our family physician and received a scold for not attending to his advice and taking the Iron more regularly, as he thinks my health demands attention. I felt inclined to tell him that I felt too much indifference to life to give myself the trouble of preserving any thing so worthless but he would have thought me madly selfish with as many children as I have to express myself in this way and I escaped with the promise that I would do better in future. During this conversation the words of Shakespeare were running through my mind, "Canst thou not minister to a mind deseased," "Pluck from the memory a rooted sorrow, and with some sweet oblivious antidote, Cleanse the foul bosom of that perilous stuff, That preys upon the heart."

1851

JANUARY 21ST

More than a month has elapsed since I made an entry in my journal, my time is so much occupied now teaching my boys at night that there is but little left to devote to writing and so many of our family are now absent that I am often engaged writing letters as we love each other too well to live apart without taking advantage of all the means of communication in our power. I must endeavour to give a short recount of the most important events that have occurred in our family history during this interval.

Our family is now more widely separated than it has ever been before. Mrs. Thorburn and her family being residents of Pensacola West Florida and the Sterlings having removed to Greensboro North Carolina where Mr. S has taken charge of a Female Academy. There are only 3 of us left here brother Jno, Sam and myself and I earnestly hope that nothing may ever occur to oblige me to change my place of residence, until I am called away from this world. My boys returned from Pr. Edw'd about the middle of Jan and right glad was I to welcome them home although I did regret the cause of their coming, and the necessity of giving up all hope of their being educated by my dear brother S. I think I am happier to have them all around me tho' it requires the exercise of great patience self-denial and industry, and I fail in all these frequently, with regard to our pecuniary affairs, prospects have rather brightened, the Mill sold well the 2nd time it was offered[38] and it is now certain that all the debts of the Estate will be paid and this has cheered me much, we must be content with a very small portion, but with the aid of boarders and my brothers help we can be kept above want and our "Heavenly Father knows what things we have need of" I can trust Him.

The winter has passed away very quickly for I have been well and constantly employed and now that mournful period is at hand when all my earthly hopes of happiness were suddenly blasted. Yesterday (April 15th, 1851) was the Anniversary of my darling little Samuel Howison's birth, I was not sorry that the sad thoughts connected with this event were interrupted by the arrival of several persons to dinner and I was kept so busy preparing for them that I had not time to dwell on gloomy subjects until night, when my pent up grief found vent in many a flood of tears. We have had nothing but rain and clouds all this week and we fear the cold north wind may have a blighting influence upon the fruit trees which have just dropped the most abundant bloom I have seen for several years.

APRIL 17TH

Dark wind-clouds cover the face of the sky, and give a sombre colouring to all beneath, this is in unison with my feelings which are mournful and dreary beyond description, as day after day passes, I live over again in thought the last days I spent blessed with the society of my dear Husband and many memories of his tender affectionate regard rush over me, and my heart aches incessantly when I know that they are lost to me forever, how often in thought do I place *him* bside my sick-bed as he was wont to stand and cheer me with lively hopeful words. I think I never saw him in better health and spirits than he exhibited during the last week of his life, not one single apprehension of the approaching thunderbolt disturbed my mind, I was engrossed with my own maladies, my care was to secure my own health and comfort and commence my active duties in the family again as soon as possible, I thought *he* would be so pleased to see me once more at the head of the table from which I had been so long absent in consequence of sickness, and I in anticipation enjoyed his glad smile of welcome, which alas! I was never more to see, this would break my heart even now to dwell on, if God had not in mercy sent me a portion of that Submission to his will which the angels have, and given me a hope of reunion in a more enduring clime than this, my mind no longer views death as it did formerly, as an entrance upon deeply solemn scenes, and a departure from much worldly happiness, from both which I shrank with an almost indefinable fear, now I look upon it as a release from toil and care, and tho I pray to be willing to endure all things and live for the sake of my children, yet my heart bounds at the idea that I shall be released one day from all responsibility to them, from this dull scene of sin and vexation and sorrow and any ransomed spirit shall soar away to the world where Jesus my Saviour sits enthroned in glory. I do not forget that dread account which is to be rendered for the "deeds done in the body" but I have humbly sincerely prayed for pardon thro' the blood of the Atoning Sacrifice, and I read in the Sacred Word of God that, "whosoever beleiveth on the name of the Son of God shall be saved" that "whosoever cometh Unto *me* I will in no wise cast out" and I know that the promises of God "are Yea and Amen in Christ Jesus."

APRIL 18TH

This has been a day of bustle and confusion, owing to the large Collection of the Sons of Temperance assembled in the town, they formed a long procession attended by numerous Marshalls on horseback and presented quite an imposing appearance. They do not appear to be generally of the upper class in Society, but, as the evil which they have united to suppress, exists more in the lower ranks than others, it is entirely proper that *they* should throw their influence against it. Mrs. S— came up and took her daughter back with her to spend the holiday which begins to-day, my kind friend Mrs. B came and sat all the afternoon with me, and Nanny's mother and Sister came in after tea and staid until 10 o'clock, so that I had not much time to myself the whole day.

APRIL 20TH

A high wind blew to-day but it was not very cold, and we attended Church where we heard a sermon from a young man named "Martin" as our pastor is confined to the house by an attack of sickness, he preached again at night but his sermon was not so well prepared as the mornings discourse, and did not interest me much.

TUESDAY THE 22ND

I had prepared to spend this day in the indulgence of the deep and heartfelt grief, which the memory of the day last year recalled, each word uttered on that morning of thoughtless security from impending evil, came vividly to mind, it was the day upon which the remains of Jno C Calhoun were brought through this place on their way to Charleston, I remember the solemn tolling of the bells as the Cars approached and left the town and as I lay reflecting upon this great Man's carreer in life,[39] I heard that well-known step across the passage, which never sounded in my ear without bringing a thrill of joy to my heart, I pushed back the curtain as my beloved husband came to the bedside, and asked him why he had not joined the procession to do honour to Mr. Calhoun, how well do I remember his reply "I came out of the store for that purpose, but when I heard the toll of the bell I thought it might make my Jenny gloomy and I would turn my steps homeward to cheer her up, as I would not be missed from the throng who were crowding to the Depot" I replied cheerfully "that I felt too well to be sad, and that relief from pain made me too glad to be depressed by any thing" he stood by me looking a little sad but with a countenance full of affection, said "you have had more suffering than usually falls to the lot of woman, but you have borne it well, and your cheerfullness under all circumstances has made my life a happy one my love" these words dwell in my mind as *almost* the last I ever heard from his lips, he came again in an hour to dine and then he spoke of my getting up next day of his welcoming me to the large Easy Chair and as he wished to appear in a suit of clothes *I liked* he gave to Aunt Eva some articles of clothing to repair, and threw them over the back of a chair and approached me with the same, playful manner, he leaned over me and gave me an affectionate kiss and then left the Room, called by the dinner bell, I never saw him more, except in his shroud. He complained soon after dinner of uneasiness about the chest, the Dr. was sent for and found him lying upon the Sofa in the dining room, recommended bathing and mustard plasters, and while in the act of applying these remedies, his noble heart stopped beating, and his pure spirit took to flight to unknown realms. My own feelings cannot be described by words a wild stunning agony, turned my heart to stone and my brain to fire. It was hours before I could be relieved by tears, the only thoughts, I well remember which passed through my mind, was a deep awful conviction of the Sovereignty of God, the Reality of eternal things and a strong desire to leave the world myself that moment. I was weak and sick and for some hours, felt sure that the separation could not be long between us, but as days rolled on and I lived *on*, I waked to an agonising sense of my loss gradually, and a perfect impatience of life took possession of me, I was roused from this by the weeping faces of my children, and Oh the heart-breaking wretchedness from which I turned back to tread my dreary way through this world without *him.* I have been blessed above others, and far above my own deserts since, but never shall my heart know real pleasure in this world more, it is best as it is, let me leave all things to G d's disposal, rest safely on his word until the end comes.

"Brompton," home of the Marye family, located near the intersection of Sunken Road and Hanover Street. (*Library of Congress*)

By the Mail from the South I received a letter from Mr. Sterling mentioning that Marion was ill and this rather diverted my thoughts from my own griefs or rather gave me causes of anxiety which in a measure neutralized them for the time.

MAY 1ST

My children have urged me to aid them in preparing for their "Queen of May" and I consented to do so chiefly with the view of interesting myself in *something,* the 'coronation' took place at Mr. Marye's beautiful residence[40] and I have rarely if ever, seen a more lovely sight, all the older girls dressed in white with blue sashes, garlands of flowers, and *happy faces,* made up a group upon the fresh Green grass which was deeply interesting and highly picturesque in its effect, the Queen and her attendants had appropriate speeches to repeat which was performed in handsome dignified style and the evening ended in a dance. I only remained to see the Coronation and felt refreshed by the sight of so many happy fair young faces without a shade of discontent upon one of them. I received a letter from my dear M— telling me of her recovery from a severe spell of illness. It was written in depressed spirits, I fear they are not doing so well as I had hoped.

MAY 11TH

Spent today at Rose Hill with the Marye's, Mrs. Ficklen and our own family, the country presents nothing but beauties to the eye now the forests are lighted up with different shades of Green, and the light winds wave them like the Sea, the wheat fields have that bright green so refreshing to the sight, before the yellow tinge begins to show the ripening of the grain, flowers are springing beneath your feet at every step, and there is enough in view from this Hillside where I stand, to fill the heart with a sense of the goodness of the Creator, in so beautifying this world of ours. Had a pleasant ride home late in the evening and heard many a glad little voice, shouting my welcome as I approached my own gate.

12TH, 13TH, 14TH

Thermometer at 89 in my passage. Clouds appeared on the evening of the last day and we had a slight rain accompanied by a high wind from the north which made so great a change in the weather that by the night of the 14th blankets were brought into requisition again.

MAY 26TH

A year has now passed since I have been keeping my own accounts strictly, and depending upon new resources for our support, I have been enabled to keep my family in great comfort and discharge all my debts and I have sufficient cause to express my gratitude to Almighty God for his goodness to me and mine, I would hereafter trust Him and serve Him with a grateful faithful heart, and would pray for continual supp— of His gracious influence to enable me to do this for when left to myself I am a wretched traitor to every thing that is good and holy.

MAY 28TH

I have again received intimation of dear M's sickness. I fear her health is broken up not to be restored again, what is to become of her young children?

1854

JANUARY 8TH

I have neglected my journal a long time, owing perhaps more to the fact that a great many of my friends have been absent and I have had an almost daily letter to write than any thing else and my time has also been very much occupied teaching school since I wrote many a sorrow has depressed me and a constant burthen of care has made me *grow old* faster than years added, but over the whole history of my life during the last three years, *such* a flood of mercy and goodness has flowed that in reviewing it I can but praise and adore that Goodness which 'has followed me'. Truly that God who has promised to befriend "the Widow and the Fatherless" has kept his word with us, and his goodness has not been confined to the supply of our temporal wants, my darling child Helen, the eldest of the numerous group which were left me to train up, has been made a subject of the Redeemer's love and is now engaged in teaching, at a distance from me it is true, but constantly watched over and guarded by her Father in Heaven of whose family she is now a true member, what more can I wish for all the rest, 'Lord make them thy children'—My dear Sister Helen has returned from Pensacola and is now living very near me, how pleasant to have her family within speaking distance. My brother Sam is also keeping house a square off, and his family form a very agreeable addition to the society of our town. Brother

"Braehead," home of Jane's brother John after he sold "Rose Hill." This historic sketch illustrates the expanse of the farm at the time of the Civil War during the "storming of Marye's Heights." (*National Park Service*)

John and his family are about to remove to the Farm[41] which will make our intercourse less frequent than I could wish, but it is a beautiful spot, upon which he will presently take up his abode, and I do so love the country, I promise myself many a pleasant walk with the children to Hazeldean.[42]

1855

JANUARY 13TH

I received a letter this morning from James enclosing one from California. My dear Ned has been unfortunate in another speculation and has lost a considerable sum of money. I feel for him and for myself too as he has aided in the support of my family since our misfortunes. Ah! How earthly hopes and expectations do cheat us, as we lose one, another springs up and promises to fully compensate for all the pain which the crushing of the last one caused us. We believe it and cling to it, only to find ourselves bourne down to the very earth in its fall. I cannot now see how my family can be sustained in the highly respectable and comfortable position we have heretofore occupied, but if we must be utterly cast down and depressed in this life Oh Father of Mercies grant that it may be for our good, that our true our eternal interests may thereby be secured, and let not a spirit of repining discontent fill my breast, but make me thankful for what Thou has already bestowed and humble in the thought of how little I deserve Thy Goodness.

1856

JANUARY 20TH

The 5th of this month a snow storm commenced, and in 24 hours the snow had fallen to the depth of 14 inches, a very severe spell of cold weather succeeded and for several days the thermometer stood several degrees below zero, the river has been frozen over, and all the skates and sleighs in town have been put to us. The Chatham bridge has been the evening resort of all the young ladies to watch the skillful evolutions of the skaters. Another snow fell on the 12th which was followed by rain and partial thaw lowering the banks of snow on each side of the walks, and making the pathway almost impassable with mud, we were hoping for a more comfortable state of things as each beautiful day shone out, and the sun beamed down upon us with something like warmth.

Saturday the 19th a large family party assembled here to dine, with a Cousin of ours from Ohio whom we have not seen for a great many years, she is very much like my Mother and I feel very near to her in consequence of this and her own intrinsic excellence thrown into the scale, we spoke of attending church to-day for the first time this year, but to my great surprise, when I drew aside the curtain this morning I found the snow falling thickly and the cleared places upon the ground covered over to the depth of at least four inches, it is now evening and still snowing rapidly so that we shall have the snow deeper here than it has been seen before in the memory of man. ▪

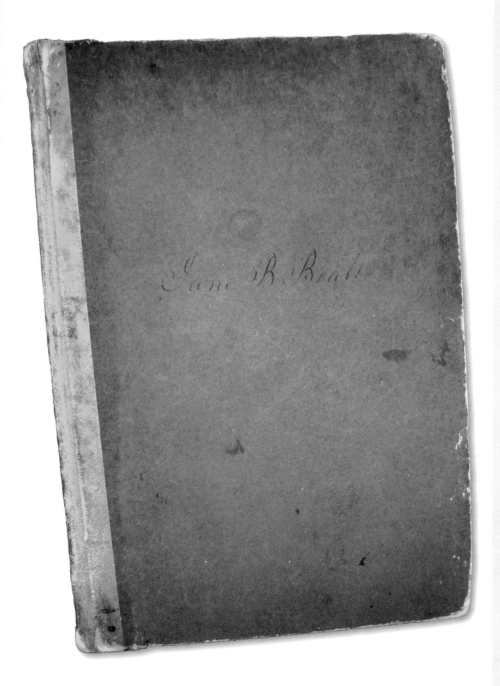

Jane Beale's name is scribed in her own hand on the cover of her journal.

About 1, o'clock there was a little cessation of the firing, and we heard my dear brother John's voice at the door, calling us to come while we could get out of the town, but when he came in and saw our condition he knew we could not walk, and get those poor sufferers past the danger in time, and after holding a hasty council with the other gentlemen it was judged too rash an undertaking for us to attempt then, brother John told us that the town was on fire in many places, a whole row of buildings on Main St were already burnt; and as my house had a shingled roof I thought we would soon be driven from it by fire also Mr Lacy left us with brother John and they could scarcely have got out of the town before the heavy Bombardment commenced again and the sound of 173 guns ~~echoed~~ in our ears, the shrieking of those Shells, like a host of angry fiends rushing through the air, the crashing of the balls

Jane's journal entry for December 11, 1862, describing her family's ordeal during the Battle of Fredericksburg. Note her correction of the word "echoed."

Bird's-Eye View of Fredericksburg, originally drawn in 1857, was updated in 1862 to reflect war damage. Jane's house is circled in black. (*Library of Congress*)

PART TWO

"A Battle Will Take Place Ere Long"

1861

JULY 23RD

Manasseh! A name associated in our minds with blood and carnage in the Bible and hereafter to fill the mind of every Southern man with deep but sad enthusiam. A great battle has been waging at Manassas Junction 20 miles from Alexandria for several days, so far with success on the side of the Southerners, but our Northern foes are strong and vindictive and we have reason to fear they may return with fresh forces and renew the attack, we know that they have great numbrs of troops in Washington City and Gen. Scott has been too long accustomed to victory to yield without a fierce struggle, we have great confidence in the wisdom and sagacity of our leaders and in the bravery and determined resolution of our army as well as in the justice of our cause, and we do not fear the final result of this war, but many a loved one must fall and many a heart throb with anguish before we can breathe the exhilerating atmosphere of freedom or feel the sweet assurance of safety and peace once more, my two sons John and Charles enlisted as Privates in a volunteer company as soon as the war commenced.[43] They are members of Capt James K. Lee's company B and belong to the 1st Reg Va Vol which is commanded by Col P T Moore of Richmond, they have been stationed at Manassas since May 26th where troops have been gradually collecting from all the States of the Southern Confederacy until Gen Beauregard has now about 60,000 under his command, on the morning of the 18th of July (last Thursday) one brigade under Gen LongStreet of S C. consisting of the 1st 11th 13th 17th Regts of Va Vol and the Washington Artillery from New Orleans were stationed at Bull Run ford the dividing line between the Counties of Pr Wm and Fairfax to intercept the progress of Northern troops under Gen McDowell: the advancing foe numbered about 7000, they were chiefly soldiers of the regular army and had strong batteries, but after a protracted struggle, our brigade drove back the Yankees at the point of the bayonet, and they retreated to their encampment at Falls Church, our loss in this engagement was reported 8 killed, 100 wounded, the enemy's loss much greater. After a night of miserable suspense, I was reliered by a telegram from my dear brother Robert, stating "that my dear boys were in the hottest of the fight but escaped unhurt" and the tide of joyous gratitude swelled to overflowing in my heart, but my happiness was of short duration, for early on Sunday the 21st we heard rumours of a general engagement at Manassas between 75,000 of the enemy's troops and all of Gen Beauregard's army. Our President Jefferson Davis with his characteristic energy and bravery started for the seat of war as soon as possible after the delivery of his message to Congress which assembled on Saturday the 20th. Upon arriving he took command of the centre division while Beauregard commanded the right wing and Johnston the left, we hear they have won a glorious but dearly bought victory, that the enemy is driven back again after losing thousands of men that our men have taken 8 of the enemy's batteries a hundred wagons and 1200 prisoners.

JULY 24TH

I have heard today that my dear ones John & Charles are again preserved and feel like exclaiming with the Psalmist "surely goodness and mercy have followed me all the days of my life" we received news that the defeat of the northern army produced a great panic in Washington City and I fear will stimulate the Government to greater exertions to conquer than ever, a great many troops passed thro' here to-day to join the army of the Potomac,[44] among them a troop of Cavalry from South Carolina,[45] it was a gallant sight, that 500 horsemen, with flowing plumes and flashing arms.

JULY 25TH

A bright pleasant day with a temperature exactly right. Reuben Gordon[46] came down having left Manassas yesterday, he had only heard of my boys, he had not been able to see them, the camp extends 7 miles and it is not easy to get within the lines, Reuben's account of the battle field is terrible, it made my heart quail to hear it, Oh when will that blessed time come when "wars shall cease."

JULY 26TH

Another delightful day, Providence has blessed our people with pleasant weather and abundant crops of grain, vegetables and fruits. It would have been far worse for the poor soldiers if they had encountered a long dry hot summer, and all our interests would have suffered from such a drowth as we usually have in July. A letter came from Helen G[47] who is at present in Fauquier. She said her uncle[48] had offered the large house at Bealeton Station[49] for the use of the wounded at Manassas, and the neighbours were to nurse them.

1862

APRIL 27TH

Fredericksburg is a captured town, the enemy took possession of the Stafford hills which command the town on Friday the 18th and their guns have frowned down upon us ever since, fortunately for us our troops were enabled to burn the bridges connecting our town with the Stafford shore and thus saved us the presence of the Northern soldiers in our midst, but our releif from this annoyance will not be long as they have brought boats to the wharf and will of course be enabled to cross at their pleasure, it is painfully humiliating to feel one'self a captive, but all sorrow for self is now lost in the deeper feeling of anxiety for our army, for our cause, we have lost every thing, regained nothing, our army has fallen back before the superior forces of the enemy until but a small strip of our dear Old Dominion is left to us, our sons are all in the field and we who are now in the hands of the enemy cannot even hear from them, must their precious young lives be sacrificed, their homes made desolate, our cause be lost and all our rights be trampled under the foot of a vindictive foe, Gracious God avert from us these terrible calamities! Rise in thy Majesty and strength and rebuke our enemies.

We heard this morning from Mr. T. Lacy[50] a sermon from the "The Lord God Omnipotent reigneth" and right gladly our hearts welcomed the truth in its grandeur and strength, when we are sinking into despondency and feeling the weakness of all human dependence.

APRIL 28TH

No news heard to-day calculated to raise our drooping spirits. New Orleans has surrendered and with it we lose the valley of the Mississippi, we are confined in narrower limits and fear that ere long we shall be completely hemmed in, our own immediate neighbourhood is now in the full beauty and promise of bloom and bud, the day has been a lovely one, I walked out to the Cemetery to have some roses and evergreens set and never did I witness a more pleasing scene, more than fifty children with their aprons filld with flowers were busily engaged ornamenting the graves of their little brothers, sisters and friends who have fallen victims during the past winter to the scarlet fever which raged here with great violence carrying off at least one hundred in its dreadful course, it was pleasant indeed to see those busy little creatures, tying wreaths, sticking the flowers in the most beautiful forms possible while others brought pitchers and watering pots of water all intent on rendering their tribute to the shrine of affection or friendship, there was no loud talking or laughing but they went about the performance of these loving duties, with a sweet solemnity, which rendered it very interesting. I watched them and two robins which were building their nest in a cedar tree near my own dear little lot until I was warned by the long slanting beams of the setting sun that it was time to turn my face homewards.

APRIL 29TH

This morning was cloudy and damp, a slight rain fell, and then the sun came out, like a true April sun as it was a friend sent me a letter from her brother on the Peninsula, in which my two sons W and C were mentioned. They were encamped at "Lebanon Church" near Yorktown, and were within two miles of the enemy and daily expecting a battle, May the arm of the Almighty be with us in this battle for the fate of our Confederacy hangs on it. We were encouraged by hearing to-day that

After the bridges were destroyed in the spring of 1862, Union soldiers crossed the Rappahannock River into Fredericksburg using pontoon bridges. (*National Park Service*)

the report of the capture of New Orleans was untrue[51] it was only feared it would be, but it had not actually, surrendered, English and French Commanders in the harbour had protested against the Federals shelling the city. The enemy across the river from us are engaged to-day in building a bridge of boats, we dread their approach as we hear they have devasted the country on the other side.

This evening proved so beautiful that I walked again to the Cemetery to have some sodding and planting completed, it was too early for the assembling of the little folks and I had the broad walk with the willow boughs waving over it all to myself, but the robins were there still busy and a mocking bird perched upon the summit of a maple tree gave me a delightful seranade.

APRIL 30TH

A drizzly rain fell all the morning keeping us indoors, engaged with sewing and writing school bills until 1 o'clock my usual hour for going in school where I remain until 3 o'clock, after dinner we attended a lecture at our church which is open now in the afternoon instead of at night as the ladies cannot go out in these perilous times after dark without an escort and all of our boys are with the army, when I came out of the Lecture room a friend gave me two letters, the sight of which made me very glad, as news from abroad and especially from absent friends was never more welcome than now, they proved to be from my youngest daughter and my Sister H. The former is at school in Greensborough, NC with Mr. Sterling and is in great distress at the idea of being cut off from home and all most dear to her, and my sister left home in a hurry to avoid the possible capture of her husband who is a Naval Officer and might be liable to be taken prisoner by our enemies as they seem to be on the lookout for any men who have taken any active part in what they are pleased to term "the rebellion." Answered both letters to-night.

MAY 1ST

The "merry month" has not been ushered in with smiles but shares the sadness and tears of her predecessor but the birds do not mind the clouds and keep up a continual song, and it does not seem so gloomy as it would be without their music. Nothing has occurred of interest to-day except visits from two of my brothers, S. to tell me of an intended trip to Richmond on bank business which at this time may be attended with danger, and requires caution and secresy, and brother J. brought me a sum of money with which to defray some debts which I have been unable to pay during this most trying and difficult year, and I feel greatly relieved by having the means furnished to defray these debts.

FRIDAY, MAY 2ND

Another gloomy day, spent within doors and without incident to vary the monotony of domestic employment.[52]

MAY 3RD

The sun shone bright and glad this morning and when Lee came with the carryall to take us out to brother John's I was very much pleased to make one of the party, the road was badly cut up by our brigade wagons and we did not enjoy the ride much but the country looked so beautiful and the situation of the house commands such a fine view that I was refreshed by the sight. The house is situated on a natural terrace the hill falling before it to an extensive and perfect level reaching to the river and now covered with a lovely carpeting of clover and young wheat, on one side a skirt of woods encloses these fair fields and on the other side sweet Hazle Run bounds the farm and in its course turns a busy mill, just under a high cliff covered with ivy, and makes a picturesque item in the scenery, beyond the run and towards the east spreads the town along the bank of the river and with its steeples and spires looks pretty in the distance, tho' it is not distinguished by architectural beauty as you approach its immediate vicinity. Behind the house there is a sufficient level for the yard and garden and then the hill rises gradually into a small mountain and is crowned by an extensive growth of fine forest trees increasing into thick woods for a mile or so back, a road over this hill leading up into the forest is often used now by persons wishing to visit the town without coming under the observation of the enemy who from their commanding position on the Stafford hills can readily discern any object approaching the town upon any of the public roads, the immediate consequence of this is that Brother John's house has become the resort of a great many who come in late and leave early, and I sometimes fear it may subject him to annoyance from the enemy searching for pickets or other suspicious characters, one of our own soldiers came while we were there and after making a sufficient change in his dress to appear as a citizen he left his horse and came on to the town, tho' we told him that it was full of Federal troops. Our ride back in the evening was in a mule cart and was not quite easy enough to lull us to sleep during its progress tho' it had the effect of producing very sound sleep afterwards.

SUNDAY, MAY 4TH

Went to church this morning and was enlightened by a very good sermon from Mr. Lacy from the words "Lo' I am with you always" we heard upon our return from church that the enemy was actively engaged building a second bridge and by night it was finished and a troop of cavalry came over and rode about and around the town. While we were seated around the supper table we heard a step and a bark of recognition from Mentor and a moment afterwards the door opened and my own dear W—[53] appeared, we were delighted to see him but rejoiced with trembling as we knew he was in danger of being captured by the enemy, he had been enabled to leave the army by Ned Howison taking his place and in compliance with his employer's desire was now on his way to resume his position at the desk in order to settle up the business. He had changed his uniform for citizen's dress in Richmond and came on with SSH from his trip of business, leaving the rail road at a point some 7 or 8 miles below this. They had walked on taking advantage of the shades of evening to steal into the quiet road through the woods and down the hill behind brother John's, he brought with him numerous letters which Robert immediately undertook to deliver and in half an hour there were many calls from the elderly gentlemen of the town to hear news of the army and of their sons and connexions, they all urged W— to lose no time in making his arrangements to leave town as the enemy were now crossing the river in numerous parties and had commenced searching houses for concealed soldiers. So I hastened to pack his trunk in order for him to leave at an early hour in the morning.

MONDAY, MAY 5TH

Rose before day to call W— and get him off before that long line of cavalry began to move through the streets, took a hasty leave of him and as I watched him disappear in the mist from the door until he disappeared in the mist and gloom of the early rainy morning my heart was filled with inexpressible anxiety for his safety, which outweighed the sorrow I felt at parting with him so soon, I sent his trunks by the milk cart and supposing he might remain all day at the Farm I wrote letters and prepared some articles which I wished him to take to Greensboro NC. As it was his purpose to go through that place on his route to Georgia. But when the children who took them out to him came back and told me he was gone I felt relieved and did not regret my failure to send the things. This evening a thousand of the enemy's Cavalry came over and scoured the country around and I began to fear for the safety of "Lee Howison" who went with my Son to meet the Cars at the depot 10 miles below this place and might meet the enemy on his return and not be able to give a satisfactory account of himself.

TUESDAY, MAY 6TH

This morning was ushered in with bright sunshine and a cold north wind making a good fire essential to comfort, I bought 2 small cart loads of wood at $3.00 each, certainly not a half cord in both together. At 10 o'clock a long line of wagons came over to take possession of some forage which was left here by our own army, the escort were well dressed and rode good horses but they do not ride like our men, they lean forward on their horses and make a prodigious clattering. About dinner time I was glad to see 'Lee' riding up, he told us of W's safe arrival with his trunk at the rail road depot, and that he had started on his return with the relief cores of our pickets, but after getting half way home, they met a Courier who informed them that the enemy was approaching in considerable force and the officer in command sent 'Lee' back as they expected to have a skirmish, he went back to Massaponax church where he met a number of people and a gentleman took him home with him to stay all night, he left his vehicle there and knowing a path through the woods he rode through early in the morning and got home safely by 10 o'clock, after parting with our pickets he heard considerable firing and soon heard reports of a fight and the retreat of our men who were in too small force to cope with a thousand. After seeing 'Lee' and having my mind relieved from its immediate burden of anxiety I went out with H & L to see an old friend whom I knew well in the happy days of my early married life and whom I have not seen during all these long weary years of trial and difficulty which followed *his* death, on our return home we saw a cavalry officer on his horse plucking flowers from a bush which spread its branches over my front palings but he rode off as we approached, I hear they are taking possession of every vacated house in the neighbourhood and I am glad I have not left my own sweet home to be desecrated.

MAY 7TH

Sent my letters by another person so it seems we are not entirely blockaded yet. Attended lecture this afternoon, and enjoyed the service very much, the text was "He shall sit as a refiner and purifier of silver," after service we walked down to see the ridge of boats built in a day by the enemy and I was surprised at the appearance of strength and perfect adaptation to its purpose which it presented, this is a wonderful people with whom we have to contend, their resources appear unlimited their energy inexhaustible.

MAY 8TH

Spent the morning reading the New York Herald containing a lengthy description of the evacuation of Yorktown by our troops and the occupation and advance of McClellan's force of a skirmish near Williamsburg etc, we have now but little of Virginia left to call our own, but we have a large army around Richmond and our side has ever been victorious when the enemy was too far from the water to be assisted by their gunboats. Nearly all our seaboard towns are now in possession of the enemy and the prospect is dark indeed around us. Nothing by Almighty power can change the force of events in our favour now. This afternoon walked out and called to see two old friends Judge Lomax and his wife and found them seated together by the fire in their chamber, both helpless she from an injury received several years back and he from old age and infirm health, he could not speak above a whisper, but his whispered words were most pleasant and cheerful and the old lady was also very cheerful. Our heavenly Father does not forsake his people in their old age and weakness.

MAY 13TH

Since my last entry my heart has been crushed with sorrow, for I have seen the death of my Son Charley[54] mentioned in the Richmond paper. He fell in the battle near Williamsburg on Monday the 5th some time between the hours of 7 o'clock and 11 AM for it was then the battle waged. Sorrow has rolled in on my soul in heavy waves, but even in this great calamity I am not left to despair, my darling precious boy left good evidence that he was "a new creature in Christ Jesus" four years ago he wept in bitterness over his sinfulness by nature and by practise and sought the Saviour with a childlike humility and deep earnestness which could not have failed to obtain the blessing he sought. And since then his Christian course has been strait onward with very great animal spirits and a keen relish for the enjoyments which this life affords. He had also a quick temper and a strong will but the spirits were subdued within the bounds of Christian moderation, the pleasures were always given up when he even supposed they conflicted with duty, the temper was curbed into the sweetest tenderest of feelings, and the strong will was only exercised in resisting the current of evil and steadily setting his face towards that which was right and good. He was the best the most affectionate and dutiful of sons to his Mother and she will ever cherish his memory with a fondness which none other can know. Our heavenly Father has taken him in his early youth (just 20 years of age) before the shadow of the sinful world had fallen deeply upon him and I can rejoice in the thought of his brightness here and follow him into the unclouded radiance of his Redeemer's presence in heaven then dry these selfish tears and force back these murmurings of the heart, and let my soul seek more earnestly than ever to drop its earthly clogs and rise into the full glad liberty of the children of God. My boy was lovely and pleasant to me and memory will revert to his dear face and sweet cheerful ways, but I will try and give him up to his Saviour, knowing that He has taken him to Himself and can provide for 'His own.'

MAY 14TH

We can hear nothing from our army or our friends, nothing which might tend in some measure to alleviate the affliction under which we are sorrowing, we are shut in by the enemy on all sides and even the comforts of life are many of them cut off, no one is allowed even to bring wood to town and we know not how we are to be supplied with the means of cooking the small amount of food we can procure. The enemy has interfered with our labour by inducing our servants to leave us and many families are left without the help they have been accustomed to in their domestic arrangements. They tell the servants not to leave, but to *demand* wages. This policy may suit them very well as it will prevent the north from feeling the great evil of a useless, expensive and degraded population among them, but it strikes at the root of those principles and rights for which our Southern people are contending and cannot be submitted to, it fixes upon us this incubus of supporting a race, who were ordained of high Heaven to serve the white man and it is only in that capacity they can be happy useful and respected. I love my servants, they are part of my family and their happiness has been my care as well as that of my own children. I can but hope that no evil influences will be brought to bear upon their minds inducing them to place themselves and me in a more unhappy position than that which we now occupy, but several of my neighbours are left without theirs and we cannot now tell "what a day may bring forth" not the least painful of our trials is that we are compelled to listen to the enemy's exultant cheers, firing of guns and loud strains of martial music in celebration of some triumph of their arms and superior numbers over our Spartan bands of which we know nothing except what their boasting tongues tell us. They invade our premises, find pretexts for thrusting their unwelcome presence upon us at every turn and are "surprised not to find more Union feeling among us" they must be most profoundly ignorant of the moral science of causes and effects to suppose that love for the 'Union' can be produced and cultivated by the persecutions to which we have been subjected, all history—all human experience teaches that those who suffer the tyranny of unjust warfare, learn to cling with a devotion to their principles that they would never have felt under milder influences and our Southern people will not be apt to form the first exception to this general rule.

In the midst of so much that is painful added to the deep sadness which environs our household, we are not left to feel ourselves forsaken, the kindness and sympathy of the dear Fred'g people was never more manifest to me than now, scarcely an hour of the day passes in which I do not receive some token of remembrance from friends, either a kind message, a lovely bunch of flowers, a waiter of nice things to eat or, best of all a visit from some dear Christian friend who talks to me of my dear boy who has fought the battle of life and so early won the crown of victory to cast at the Redeemer's feet. Surely there has been great mercy mingled with this stroke, there should be no murmurings in my heart but an humble acquiescence in the Divine will and a heartfelt reliance upon Him who "doeth all things well."

MAY 15TH

A rainy season has set in and keeps us out of the garden, where we had some recreation and exercise. No wood can be got and I am trying to bring my mind to consent to cutting down some of the old trees which have long extended their sheltering branches over my yard, none shall go but those that are early worn out with age and hard winters, and even they, I would see wholly dead, before I would give the order to cut them down, for my children have played beneath their shade and they are endeared to me by many tender associations.

A letter from our former Pastor (Rev A A Hodge)[55] came to my hand to-day, it was addressed to his "friends in the church" and was full of sympathy with us in our present afflictions. I do not know why I have never mentioned him in my journal before for he is very near my heart and was with us a most beloved and honoured Pastor for nearly 6 years, and was only induced to leave us by the civil war breaking out, and fearing that he would be cut off from his aged father and all his friends at the north. I do not beleive he took sides with our enemies in their political opinions, or approves of the war which is waged against us. His mind is of the highest order and we shall never forget the words of burning eloquence which he poured forth from the pulpit, in pressing the great truths of the Bible home upon the consciences of his audience, and still less shall we forget his affectionate personal intercourse, during his stay two of my children were hopefully converted and united with the church, and I have reason to hope that his influence upon them all was very good. The dear one whom we mourn was connected by the closest intimacy with him and I have no doubt owed his early formed religious principles to our Pastor's instrumentality.

MAY 17TH

Nothing has occurred of much interest since my last entry, we have sent a letter to my niece in Norfolk with the hope of hearing something in reply about the fight at Williamsburg, as we can hear nothing from Richmond, many kind friends have called to express their sympathy with me in my great sorrow, our near neighbour Mr. Wm F Broaddas[56] Pastor of the Baptist church in this place came yesterday and by his affectionate Christian words and his earnest prayer did much to soothe my aching heart. He is I beleive a true servant of Christ and I greatly value his friendship for me and mine.

The Home of William F. Broaddus, pastor of the Baptist Church, at 1106 Princess Anne Street.

MAY 19TH

Another Sabbath has passed and we are still at home in our suspense and sorrow. No mourning can be procured and the family must go on with stricken hearts but no outward symbol of grief for the dear one gone from us, never more to return and gladden us with his presence, but we will remember the words of St. Cyprian "We may not here below put on dark robes of mourning, when they above have put on the white robes of glory."

I am constantly receiving visits of kind sympathy from friends, and have been enabled to obtain an abundant supply of wood from brother John for which I am very thankful.

MAY 20TH

A letter was received in town last night which stated that the report of my Charley's death had been contradicted in Richmond and that the last that had been heard of him was that he was severely wounded and had been left in Williamsburg to fall into the hands of the enemy with many other poor wounded prisoners. I have not been much relieved by this, as the situation of my son seems more distressing to me now than when I thought of him before. He must have been dreadfully wounded or he would have exerted every nerve to go with our army when they left there rather than be left to the tender mercies of a ruthless foe, and that he may have suffered on for days before released by death, is agony to me. I sometimes hope that he may have been taken by some kind person before the enemy got there and may have been suffered to remain at a private house instead of being carried to a crowded hospital. I have written to Gen'l Patrick[57] to ask for some information and if I hear that my son is alive, I will if possible go to him by Fortress Monroe.

MAY 26TH

Received a letter from my dear brother R on the 22nd, dated the 15th in which he stated that he had certain information of the death of my Charley from 'Lieut Robbins'[58] of Co B. and I quote from his letter, "Charley was unhurt until the last of the action, but all the officers being wounded he had to take the lead and was cheering on the men for a final and successful charge when he was struck by a ball in the breast and fell, his friend Lieut R ran to him but he was unconscious and died almost instantly." My son—I could weep torrents of tears for thee but something within stills me, there is deep comfort under this swelling tide of sorrow in the thought that not even "the sword" or death can separate us from the love of God in Christ Jesus and that now thou art gone into his immediate presence, gathered safely into the upper fold of the Good Shepherd.

I have been much employed lately nursing my Sister Nanny[59] who is ill, and having lost one of her servants, needs the attention of her friends especially. It has been good for me to be thus employed as it has occupied my attention not leaving so much time to dwell on my own troubles. A large force of the enemy moved from this place yesterday evening and we are comparatively quiet today.[60] The design is no doubt to surround our Capital and take possession of it but they have a large army to overcome before that can be done and I humbly but most earnestly pray the interposition of our Heavenly Father on our behalf at this important crisis.

MAY 28TH

We are now entirely cut off from all communication with our friends South and only hear what is transpiring in a general way from the Northern papers, the latest of which gives an account of a recent victory of our Gen'ls Jackson & Ewell over "Banks" the Ex Gov of Mass. The latter retreated into Maryland, and that part of the valley of Va is thus relieved from the presence of the invader. We hear many rumors of portions of our army appearing suddenly in unexpected places, which have been evacuated some time ago, and this gives us some hope that dear old Virginia is not to be deserted. I know that her sons are willing to offer up their lives upon her altar, I pray that the sacrifice may be accepted and her calamities averted. We hear of serious trouble in Baltimore attacks of the Union party upon those who are known to sympathise with the South. This city has long and justly held the title of 'Mob Town.' Maryland must now do one of two things, give up her slaves and unite herself to the Free Soil platform of the North, or determine to fight it out with the South, the action of the US Congress leaves her no middle ground to occupy.

JUNE 1st

Either the success of Jackson or some other cause has induced an entire change in the plans of the enemy as the whole force which left here last Sunday & Monday have returned marched directly through the town crossed the river and taken up their line of march towards the Northern part of the State, we had McCall's division of about 15,000 troops left here until yesterday when infantry, artillery and cavalry took their departure, we heard early in the day that a considerable force of our men were very near the town, and as the river was rising rapidly under the influence of the continued rain, the enemy made some haste to get themselves, their baggage wagons and beeves safely to the other side before they left however they managed to raise a considerable panic among our people especially the blacks by threatening to shell the town in the night and the consequence was the removal of a great many and the excitement of all who remained all of mine rushed in about 10 o'clock last night in great alarm, and it was with difficulty I could quiet their fears, I succeeded to some extent at last, but I found them in such a state this morning as to give me very little hope of their remaining at their post of duty. The Federal army has abolished slavery wherever it has gone and certainly if their design was to punish us by subjecting us to every inconvenience and indignity which an entire rupture of our domestice relations was certain to produce they have succeeded. We have heard of a battle in Hanover,[61] another at Mechanicsville in New Kent, but nothing certain as to results, we only the Fed'l Newspapers, which always claim victory, but we receive their assertions with *many* grains of allowance. I do long to get one truthful account without any of the false colouring which Northern editors daub their pictures with.

I was disappointed in not being able to go to church this morning by the rain continuing but I spent the time in reading and teaching my youngest Son. Julian (the one next older) has been very sick this week and I have spent so much time with him and with Nanny that I have not had much opportunity for either reading or writing. I am also part of every day in school and am very much interested in the progress of my little girls.

JUNE 3D

It has become very warm suddenly and we have frequent thunder storms, nothing of much interest has occurred here, but we read in the Baltimore papers that a battle has been fought on the banks of the Chickahominy, and certainly 'McClellan's' report of it to 'Stanton' the US Lee of War does not declare that they have obtained a victory, they have every advantage of numbers, equipments, arms and appointments. A balloon was used to ascertain all the movements of our army and a telegraphic apparatus connected with it communicated all the intelligence thus gained to the Com'r thus enabling him to send reinforcements at the right time to the right point, they have a corps of skilfull artisans accompanying each department of the army who can rebuild rail road bridges and construct other bridges in the shortest time, and they certainly lose nothing for want of skill and energy in the accomplishment of their design of conquering the South, but the determined bravery of our troops, the strong motives which nerve their arms, under their wise officers, often scatter the splendid arrangements of the enemy like chaff before the wind, May God grant that it may have been so in this last important engagement. McClellan admits that a whole division of his army under 'Casey' was routed, their guns and baggage all taken by our troops, but he says that our army was afterwards repulsed, we long to hear more.

JUNE 6TH

I have been sick for several days and unable to write, it has rained constantly and all the Yankee bridges have been washed away, the cars can no longer come into the town, but we hear the whistle of the locomotive from the other side of the river and we get a few Northern papers brought over in a boat, they give us no farther information concerning the battle of the Chickahominy the storm seems to have interrupted the telegraphic wires. Mr. Lacy spent yesterday evening here. I was too unwell to see him but the family told me that he appeared very despondent in relation to our cause. Certainly the evacuation of the strong fortification at 'Corinth' by 'Beauregard' is disheartening as it proves weakness in some vital part, but we do not know what motives may have actuated our brave, wise General and we must trust him and hope for the best.

JUNE 9TH

I was occupied all day Saturday in writing letters to go by a messenger who was paid by the gentlemen here to go through the enemy's lines and get some news of our army and particularly of our citizens who were engaged in the recent fights near Richmond, he started, but since he was left 3 newspapers and several letters have by some means found their way into our town from Richmond and from them we learn that our army has whipped 'McClellan' in two engagements, both sides have lost considerably, but none of our immediate friends have been either killed or wounded.[62] Our army is in fine spirits, confident of final success, we have been fortunate in getting an abundant supply of fine arms into a Southern port recently and a cargo of ice has been by some means procured for the Hospitals in Richmond which will greatly ameliorate the sufferings of the wounded, we are very very thankful for this "goodness and mercy" which has "followed us." Yesterday I attended church for the first time since my dear Charley's death and felt almost strangely calm and quiet in mind, my thoughts would continually revert to the sweet beloved face which smiled upon me from the corner of the pew but a few Sabbaths before, but it did seem to shine down upon me from heaven so now that I could not grieve may God Almighty give me grace so to walk that I may be prepared to join him in that happy home above, in the evening as I was seated with my two youngest boys and my two little nieces reciting the Shorter Catechism to me, Sam came in with his children and soon after Betty Lacy came in with 4 of hers and the class had to be speedily dismissed as there was no longer any chance of quiet, I got some alphabets and set the little ones to spelling for their amusement and we sat down to talk with unusual cheerfulness over the news we had received from Richmond.

JUNE 16TH

My time has been devoted to my poor Nanny for a week, her illness seems to increase and her head is so violently affected that she cannot bear the noise of her children, attention to them and to her has occupied me entirely if it were possible to get her mother here or one of her sisters how glad I should be the comfort of their presence would do more towards her restoration than any thing else but this miserable way has brought all manner of evils, in its train not the least of which is the embargo laid upon intercourse with friends, we can neither see or hear from any one even a few miles from us, our rail-rds are destroyed bridges burned and we can have no communication outside of the town except by the reluctant permission of the enemy and we hate to ask favors of the ill-natured Provost Marshal.[63] They have been employing themselves

The Union occupation of Fredericksburg in the spring of 1862 brought annoyance and outrage, and local women often resisted fiercely. They could not know that the annoyances of spring would turn far more destructive the following December. (*National Park Service*)

The Lacy's city home on Chatham Hill overlooking the town of Fredericksburg, as it appeared during the Union occupation. It is now the headquarters of the National Park Service. (*Library of Congress*)

during the past week arresting every one whom they have any reason to suspect of conveying letters or papers, and even women have been taken up. Mr. Horace Lacy[64] having ventured to his country set 15 miles from this place sent for his family to join him there which they had scarcely done when a body of cavalry rode up and tore him away from his happy home circle to carry him North to some gloomy prison. This is a time of persecution and of trial, may God have mercy upon us and shorten it "for the elect's sake."

JUNE 18TH

Yesterday was a day of suffering. I went around to nurse Nanny as usual but my head ached, and it soon increased to such a degree that I was compelled to return home and lie down, leaving her to the care from my dear Minnie, from Will, and from RRH and tho' were all full of grief for the loss of our dear precious Charley, they were received with thankfulness and gave me great comfort. There is also much reason to hope from the news we have heard that the army is gaining decided advantages over the enemy and that our cause may finally triumph.

JUNE 21ST

Constantly occupied going to and fro between home and Sam's residence I have had no time to write except a short letter to my dear niece 'Bell McIntosh' who is in affliction on account of the death of her husband who was mortally wounded upon one of the gun boats in the fight at New Orleans. Helen and Lucy went yesterday to brother John's to stay all night and when I returned from a late visit to Nanny, home looked rather gloomy and deserted. I did not like to come into the dark house and seated myself in the porch, but had not remained there long when I saw through the

The Bankhead family lived at the "Steamboat House" at 1116 Prince Edward Street.

over hanging branches of shrubbery a figure approaching who turned into the gate and proved to be my old friend Mrs. Bankhead. She staid with me until 10 o'clock and her animated discourse concerning the recent events of the war enlivened me very much. To-day I have been very busy picking currants to make jelly, putting up summer curtains and making other arrangements for the warm season, and after these were finished I sat down to rest and mend some of Nanny's children's clothes, the papers contain but little news to-day, in the evening about sunset, Mr. Rogers the Methodist minister called in and while I was sitting in the parlour talking with him our own Pastor Mr. Lacy came, he told me he had been on a visit to Greenwood and found Betty and the children well and more cheerful and hopeful than he expected. Soon after a mule cart drove to the door and I saw Helen G. Lee and little Nanny seated in it. Mr. R— went out with a chair to help H— out of the homely vehicle and was much amused to find her encompassed with baskets of eggs and buckets of strawberries, like a regular huckster.

JUNE 22ND

A sweet peaceful Sabbath morning I was glad there was nothing to prevent me from attending divine service and got ready early to go but the church was so full of Fed'l soldiers that I thought at first the trial would be too great for me to bear, but their deportment was quiet and reverential, and I almost forgot they were our enemies, I was very much interested in the sermon, it was about "the shadow of a great rock in a weary land" and seemed to come home to our tried hearts with a most soothing effect. We heard when we came out of church that we might be able to send letters to the South and we thought it not wrong to employ a portion of the sabbath in writing to our friends but before we finished, we heard the messenger had gone off in the night and we were sorry to have missed the chance.

JUNE 23RD

On my way to see Nanny I met Mollie Patten and Madge Chew, the former told me she was going to Orange Ct House to-morrow and would take my letters, and so I hastened home to write three letters to Willie, Minnie and John, but after all, she could not take them as she was required to give an assurance that she would take no letters, when her passport was obtained, and so I was again disappointed. We had a terrible storm with thunder and lightning this evening and a house in which a number of soldiers were assembled was struck and two of them stunned, but afterwards recovered, another one met his death by being thrown from a horse and fell with his head upon the curb stone.

JUNE 24TH

The storm of yesterday continued all night, causing the river to rise and the bridges to wash off again. Our river like the rest of rebeldom will not submit to Yankee rule and continually rises in opposition, we wish Jackson was in the neighbourhood to take advantage of the present state of things and drive the enemy from our midst.

JUNE 25TH

A cool delightful day after the rain. Brother John sent for the children and after they left I wrote a long letter to my childrens nurse Aunt Eva Young[65] in Detroit, in the afternoon attended at our lecture room and heard a very pleasant short discourse from Mr. Lacy from the text, "When a man's ways please the Lord, He maketh even his enemies to be at peace with him." After the sermon I walked towards home with the widow of a deceased clergyman who is here living in a family near us, and who seems a lonely sorrowful woman. I listened to her tale of distress, and while I felt very sorry for her I was inwardly thankful that I was surrounded with a family of good affectionate children and numerous relatives and friends. I called to see Nanny for half an hour and then with my little boys walked out to the cemetery where I arrived just in time to see the lovely sunset, with the long shadows resting upon the quiet graves, the Microfilla Roses and Chinese Honeysuckle filled with the soft evening air with the most delicious perfume and every thing was so sweet and attractive that we lingered there till quite late.

JUNE 26TH

A visit from Mr. Lacy occupied a good deal of the morning and the rest of the day has been spent in sewing for the boys, was very glad to send my letters at last by a man who brought me wood and who promised to take them to the Bowling Green and mail them there. Heard a report to-day that a courier had passed thro' town on his way to Richmond with despatches from the French Minister containing the information that France and Belgium had acknowledged our independence, but this is about the 20th time that such reports have been circulated and it no longer excites us to gladness to hear them, I am distressed to hear that two of our greatest Generals are incapable of duty upon the field, Gen'l Joe Johnston from a wound in the shoulder received in the battle of June 1st at Fair Oaks and G. W. Smith has had an attack of paralysis, I fear their places cannot easily be supplied.[66]

JUNE 27TH

Broke up school for the summer and received many little tokens of affection from my pupils both to Helen G and myself, consisting of embroidered handkerchiefs, cologne bottles, cream pitchers and other things not very valuable in themselves but made very precious by their being gifts of love. Several persons called in the evening, among them Mrs. W P Conway[67] who has just returned from the North after a year's absence. She talked a great deal but I could not learn any thing either of her own opinions or of those she had been with but she has not my full confidence as a true Southern woman.

JUNE 28TH

Spent the day in my usual Saturday's employments, mending and assorting clothes.

JUNE 29TH

A rainy morning prevented my going out to church and I spent the time as usual with my boys, attended church in the afternoon and heard a good sermon from Mr. Rogers[68] the Methodist minister who preached in our church to quite a large congregation, and a prayer from Mr. Broaddas. These Union meets tend very much to promote good feeling in the churches, a great many Fed'l soldiers attend and listen with apparent interest and I hope they too may be influenced to a better state of feeling. After night came on and the candles were lit we heard some one calling at the front gate and Bob went out and brought in Grey Doswell with a Despatch which he had copied from one received to-day at Beaver Dam (a depot on the Central RR) stating that "our army had routed McClellan and the latter was in full retreat towards 'White House' on the Pamunkey." We received this news with tremulous joy it may not be true and if it is, who may have fallen in the struggle, very dear to us!

JUNE 30TH

A day of restless anxiety eagerly looking for news, and afraid to believe all we heard, the Northern papers contain nothing but a "report of painful news from Wash'n" we hear from various persons coming in town from the counties below us that a fierce battle has certainly been raging, that McClellan's right wing has been forced to give way and retreat towards the Pamunkey, that the attack was first made by Longstreet's Division on Wednesday and renewed every day until Saturday when our invincible Stonewall Jackson came upon the retreating army and cut off the York river rail road thus separating the two wings of the Fed'l army.

JULY 5TH

Nearly a week of intense anxiety has passed and we are still speculating on the probable condition of the two armies. Information from both leads us to the certain knowledge that the Fed'l army has been forced to retreat from its position in front of Richmond, and that McClellan is endeavouring to gain the banks of the James, we are very very grateful for the victory which ensures the safety of our Capitol, but it has been purchased at so heavy an expense, such a terrible loss of life, that it seems to be no time for exultation. O heavenly Father grant that the liberty gained by such sacrifices may be blessed, not only to us but to the world in the advancement of the Redeemer's kingdom.

JULY 6TH

Attended church this morning and listened with great interest to a sermon from 2nd Tim 4th Chap 7 & 8th verses, a great many of the Fed Soldiers were present and many of our congregation absent, we have some hope that the army is about to remove from here as we saw many ambulances filled with sick soldiers passing to the Depot, and we know this is the first step towards an evacuation. Brother Jno and his family dined with me to-day.

JULY 7TH

I commenced the morning by writing a letter to a lady[69] in New York who was once my teacher, and has proved herself my warm friend by many acts of kindness since, she married a very wealthy man but as he belongs to the Black Republican party, we have as a matter of course had no communication since this war commenced, I only wrote to her now to bespeak her kind offices in favor of two English ladies who are about to leave here with a view of returning to England by one of the New York Steamers and will probably need the aid of a gentleman in their embarkation. After this I sewed steadily to keep myself from fretting about the heat which has been intense, towards evening a fine breeze sprung up accompanied with slight rain and very much improved the state of things, the newspapers (all Northern) give us farther particulars of the retreat of McClellan and the fighting from day-to-day during its progress and they let us a little more into the Northern mind on the subject, many of the leading papers acknowledging the humiliation they feel under the defeat and calling for a change of leaders as well as a change of policy.

JULY 8TH

Another very hot day, the thermometer reached to 95° in some situations but I scarcely think it could have been so high in any part of my house, Sam sent me a bundle of Southern newspapers containing accounts of the battles before Richmond from June 25th and I have spent most of the day in poring over them catching one familiar name after another engaged in the numerous fights and ah! How many among the lists of killed and wounded, a Northern M C may well speak of "poor bleeding Dixie" now tho' I suppose he no longer dares to do it. We have been uneasy all day on account of the absence of Charley's dog "Mentor," who has been missing since Sunday evening and whom we at first supposed had followed brother John's family home on that evening, but hearing he was not there, we fear he has been stolen away, and that we may never recover him. I cannot bear to think of losing him, he was my dear Charley's companion in many a hunt and a great favorite with him, the very last visit he paid me in April, his coming was first announced by Mentor, and I shall never forget his demonstrations of joy at the sight of his beloved master.

We heard a report this evening that 'Halleck's' army from the far South West had reached Pennsylvania by way of the Miss & Ohio rivers and I fear its advance into Va. and more fighting. I am longing for the European powers to interfere, nothing else will stop the war.

JULY 9TH

Hotter than ever, and still dry, if we suffer from it how much worse it is for our poor soldiers, in thick clothing and exposed to the burning rays of the sun. While I was dressing I was glad to hear 'old Mentor's' well known bark and soon after Bob knocked at my room door to tell me of his return, he appeared weary and hungry and had evidently swam the river and so we came to the conclusion that he had been carried off by some of the northern soldiers and, like any other prisoner, took the first opportunity to escape. A man came up from Richmond to-day bringing newspapers to the 7th the statements of the whole plan operations against McClellan is highly interesting but the execution of a part at least failed and this failure may cause the whole work to be done over again, when if it had been accomplished it would have saved much bloodshed and suffering in the future we cannot however yet judge fairly as all the points in the case are not perfectly known, and we must be satisfied with knowing that Richmond is saved for the present, and we must trust to Almighty God for the future.

JULY 10TH

Mist and cloud with a slight breeze, the change from the burning heat of yesterday is delightful, my dear Lucy bought me a dress and we sat down to make it and sewed diligently until the newspapers arrived when one is always *detailed* to read aloud they contain many things to make us hope that our enemies are getting tired of the war and that the European powers will soon interfere to prevent its continuance, as for the Southern people they can take no steps to put a stop to it, they must fight as long as they are invaded many express strong wishes that England may be compelled to go to war with the United States and thus be the instrument to avenge the deep wrongs which that Government has inflicted upon us, but I cannot help feeling that peace will be so important to our young nation, just struggling into existence and my heart so sickens at the thought of any more blood shed, that I would willingly forego the vengeance in this life and let the great Judge of all the earth deal with the offenders according to the everlasting principles of justice which support His throne, I confess this subject is too great for me to deal with and am rejoiced that One so great and good, "rules among the armies of heaven and the inhabitants of this world."

JULY 11TH

The sun shines through mist and has the appearance which it presents in Indian summer, the deep red disc showing plainly, it was so pleasant that Lucy and I determined on a trip to the stores to try and find some goods which were very much needed, we were quite successful, and I was glad to find that our *capture* had not been the source of unmixed evil to us as the known cupidity of the northerners has induced the introduction of many articles which we poor blockaded Southerners needed and which we readily pay our money for tho' we have to submit to a discount of 40 percent upon our Southern notes, we dislike this very much but necessity has no law and I do not admire *naked martyrdom*, so we abuse the Yankees to our heart's content, but buy their goods still, we got no papers to-day except one from Phil'a which only contained the news we had read yesterday.

JULY 12TH

Another pleasant day, the temperature very nearly right, the *rain crow* as the boys call it has been croaking in the trees all day but has cried in vain for no rain has fallen, I have been busy all day preserving blackberries and mending old clothes, the blockade obliges us to be very economical in dry goods and indeed every thing is so high that "do without" is the common household maxim now, cotton goods which we have always bought so cheap and had in such comfortable abundance are now scarce and high; calicoes which we formerly bought at 10 cts now sell at 37½, and we cannot procure many articles we need at all, so we turn the old ones, and by constant altering and repairing we manage to keep decent. We got the newspapers again to-day and were shocked to see that Congress (of the US) had passed a bill to arm the Slaves surely Satan has been allowed to hold complete dominion in the North lately and this his last device for vengeance is the crowning point of his wicked design against us, we must trust in God's mercy to avert from us this great evil with which we are threatened.

SUNDAY, JULY 13TH

We had a crowded church to-day as there was no service in the Episcopal or Baptist churches and with parts of three congregations and more than a hundred Yankees

Princess Anne Street, the cultural heart of Fredericksburg, during the war. The Baptist Church at the intersection of Princess Anne and Amelia Streets is in the distance. (*Library of Congress*)

our church was full. Mr. L sometimes offends our taste by rather more attention to the Yankees than we like to see paid, but preaches very good sermons to make up for it.

SATURDAY, JULY 19TH

The week has been spent in steady work, enlivened by continual reports of our successes against the enemy contained in their own newspapers and brought from our Capital by persons returning from visits to their relatives after the battles. Let me enumerate. Curtis' army defeated by Hindman in Arkansaw, Vicksburg successfully defended and the Fed'l gunboats smashed by the 'Ram,' from Yazoo river. Murfreesboro in Te. retaken and the Fed'l army under T Crittendon captured. Morgan's successful raid through a portion of Ky. and now we are beginning to feel the fearful excitement which attends the movement of hostile armies in our own neighbourhood. We hear that a portion of Pope's army have penetrated as far as Gordonsville and destroyed a portion of the Central RR at that point, and also that our own General 'Stonewall' Jackson is not far off with a large army the advanced guard of which must come up with the enemy very soon if it has not already reached Gordonsville. The army around our town is evidently making preparations for a rapid move as they have been busily engaged for several days moving their sick, and their stores across the river. Went down street this morning and found the whole town alive with business, extensive purchases of groceries and dry goods going on, as if in preparation for the close blockade which must ensue ere long. Saw a great many friends, all of whom told me they had lost their servants. I was thankful mine still remained and are good and faithful. I had had an opportunity of writing to my dear little Minnie and to Robert in Richmond and was truly glad to avail myself of it.

JULY 23RD

The first news we heard this morning was that four of our citizens Mr. T Barton, Mr. Knox, Mr. C C Wellford and Mr. Gill had been arrested and sent north we have no information why, the recent orders of Stanton and Gen'l Pope[70] make it appear that we are not to be treated with the least leniency hereafter, our Provost Marshal has been changed because he was "too kind to the rebels" and they are now doing every thing they can to persecute and annoy us. All the stores in town were closed to-day to prevent us from getting our supplies and they have been sending their wagons around to every body's farm in the neighbourhood taking their hay and other products. I am afraid poor brother John will have nothing left for his winter supply.

William Street during the war. This was Fredericksburg's main entrance from the west, and the site of many businesses and warehouses. (*National Park Service*)

AUGUST 11TH

I have been prevented from writing for 3 weeks by an attack of sickness which has caused me severe suffering, during all this period we have had the weather intensely hot and dry and have been so closely shut in by the enemy's line of pickets that we have not been able to hear one word from our dear South except the garbled statements their own papers contain nor to procure any articles from the country around upon which we have been accustomed to depend for our comfortable subsistance our gardens afford us a few vegetables, and Julian's hens supply us with the eggs we need, our hydrants have stopped running and we are almost entirely dependant upon the pump in the neighbourhood we feel greatly depressed under these evils and cannot avoid casting our thoughts forward to the winter that is before us with its accumulated horrors of want and difficulty, no food left in the country no fuel to be obtained except at enormous prices and with great difficulty. This is indeed a time when we feel especial need of the grace of God to keep our hearts from unbelief and impatience.

I have received one letter lately which was indeed like a stream in the desert to my weary thirsting heart, it was from my dear friend Mr. Hodge and related chiefly to our great bereavement, and was full of affectionate sympathy, and true consolation.

If I could only hear from my children who are absent from me, it has been so long since I did that I know not what may have occurred to them, but our enemies are especially careful to let no letters either go or come from the South now and there is no telling when this close blockade will cease.

AUGUST 18TH

The rain and high wind of last Wednesday have been followed by a season of cool pleasant weather, indeed the nights are cold enough to render an additional coverlid necessary, and the mornings so chilly that we resort to the sunny walks in the garden for comfort, we are still prisoners and get no news from our own especial friends in the South but the Northern newspapers have been received and read with great interest. A battle was fought on the 9th at "Slaughter's mountain" Culpeper Cty[71] not more than 33 miles from this place between a part of 'Pope's' army under 'Banks' and a part of our army under 'Ewell' the northern side, as usual, claim a victory and 'Halleck' sends a congratulatory Despatch to Pope on account of his "Brilliant success" but all the statements from the battle field tell a very different story to me, and the large number of killed, wounded and prisoners on the Federal side, would surely not indicate a *great victory*. Our army have certainly fallen back this side of the Rapidan river and are now stretched along the line of the Central RR but most of the force near Gordonsville. We *beleive* that our sagacious Gen'l Jackson will choose his own ground for fighting the decisive battle with Pope and the advance to Slaughter's Mt. was only to induce Pope to concentrate his force and advance across the river. How strange and sad the change over the face of that lovely country through which I have so often travelled in earlier days. The beginning of the South Western Range of mountains is marked by high hills, beautiful smiling valleys, through which the eye can trace the course of the Rapidan for miles. I have watched the sunlight gradually fading from the face of broad green fields and sinking behind one of those mountains, and I have been wakened by the cry of the hounds and rushed to the window of the dear old '*yellow room*' at Somervilla[72] to look out upon one of the loveliest scenes that ever pleased the eye, the Sun rising behind the hills on the opposite side of the river and deepening the shadows of the tall forest trees on the side of old "Clarke's mountain" the sweet fields on the river bank still in deep shade, the stream itself just catching at intervals the bright rays of sunlight and sending back its glittering reflection through the fringe of beech trees and willows which lines its banks, and presently my eye would catch a view of the steep path up the mountain's side between a field and a wood, upon which the hounds were advancing in full cry followed by the huntsmen. And what strange peculiar pleasure the sound of the horn and the cry of those hounds infused into my childish mind. Now those hills and valleys echo to the deadly sound of guns and the clash of arms and those fair fields are trodden down and desolated with the march of great armies. We have no sweet retirement, no peaceful shady homes, no sense of rest and safety in Virginia now, all our sacred things are desecrated, all our pleasant friendly intercourse interrupted and even the dear family reserves of grief and affection are spread open to the view of scoffing enemies, dear old Mother of States! How many of thy gallant sons now rest upon thy bosom in their last sleep, while thy daughters weep for the slain, and mourn even more sadly for the evils which have come upon the living.

AUGUST 19TH

We are trying to begin our preparations for the mournful season that is before us and I sent into brother John's woods to get my first supply of fuel, but the messenger came back with the account that all the wood which was cut by our men last spring had been carried off by the Yankees and a new supply had to be cut before I could get any. It is now $10 per cord and I do not know what we may have to pay when the cold season comes.

Mr. Rogers came and spent the morning with us and we had some music on the piano and L— sang some sweet songs. In the afternoon attended lecture and afterwards called to see Miss E Lomax whom we found in a very happy frame of mind, and we listened to her pious words with great interest. She seems to feel as if she were very near Heaven and longs very much to be there. I wish I could feel as well prepared for the great change as I think she is.

AUGUST 26TH

We have been in a state of anxiety for a week, hearing guns every day and knowing that the two armies arrayed against each other, were about to meet in another battle more deadly perhaps than any hitherto waged. We have heard nothing, except that the Fed'l army under 'Pope' have fallen back from Culpeper Ct H and have crossed the river into Fauquier. We know nothing of the movements of our own army and can only judge by those of the enemy, that they are threatened by a large force. Our town seems to have gone into new hands and 'Burnside' holds sway here now. Numerous pickets are stationed around the town within half a mile and all our pleasant walks are interrupted. We manage to get up the lane around by Kenmore and through the field to the Monument where we have a pleasant view of the surrounding country, tho' this affords but a short walk.

"Kenmore," original home of the Lewis family, located at 1201 Washington Avenue.

AUGUST 31ST

The last day of the month has come and we are not yet relieved from the presence of our enemies as we have hoped to be. They have certainly been making preparations to evacuate the town for several days and we have seen such brilliant fires at night on the hills of Stafford that we think they must be burning army property which they do not wish to fall into the hands of the Southern army. On Friday afternoon (the 29th) there was an alarm given that a troop of southern Cavalry was approaching the town from the plank road. Consternation spread thro' the town as the Yankee army was immediately drawn up in battle array at the head of all the streets leading out west, and we thought that if our troops carne up there would be a hard fought battle in the streets. Preparations were made to burn or blow up the bridges and the cannon were put in position to command the town, the Yankee soldiers were cursing and swearing that if they had to retreat they would shell the town, and all this alarmed the negroes so much that there was a perfect stampede across the bridges and hundreds of poor frightened creatures with their children in their arms rushed away from their homes to spend the night on the cold ground and to starve all next day. Mine were not proof against this terrible excitement and two of them left, this caused me much distress as they have been good servants and besides being useful were endeared to me by ties of affection. I have one left, one who was raised by my dear Mother and has been like one of my family so long that I could scarcely bear to part with her. I hope she will not go, but she seems to be so wild and excited that I cannot depend upon her. Helen G—, Lucy and myself do the work as yet with the aid of the boys and thus devided we have not found it very arduous.

SEPTEMBER 1st

After writing the last entry in my journal yesterday, several exciting events occurred, the rain poured down all the morning but ceased about noon, and after dinner we

A wartime view of the ruined Chatham Bridge, linking William Street with Stafford County. (*National Park Service*)

went to church to hear Mr. Lacy. We found crowds at the corners of the streets, and some unusual excitement prevailing and we saw clouds of smoke rising from the encampments on the opposite side of the river. We went on to the Baptist church where we found rather a scant audience. We had a short sermon, and when we came out we walked down several squares toward the bridges. Every thing indicated an immediate departure the guard was drawn up in line, the horses and wagons packed at Headqrters, cavalry officers rode up and down giving orders, company after company of pickets marched into town from the different roads and joined the regiment at the City Hall, ambulances with the sick moved slowly through the streets and as we stood watching we saw the Officer who acted as Provost Marshal of the town ride by with his Adjutant, and in a few moments the command was given to march and away went infantry down one street, cavalry down another to the bridge. It was very quietly done, there was no music, no drum, not a voice broke upon the air except the officers "forward march." It was certainly rather difficult to repress the exultation of the ladies as they stood in groups along the streets, but strong feeling was at work and perhaps it was easier to repress any outward manifestation of it than if it had been slighter.[73] I felt glad to be relieved of the presence of the enemy, and to be freed from the restraints of their power, glad to be once more within Southern lines and to be brought into communication with our own dear people. But the great *gladness* was that the evacuation of Fred'g showed that they had been defeated up the country and could no longer hold the line of the Rappahannock. And this gave such strong hope that Virginia might yet be freed from the armies of the invader. We had scarcely reached home when a thundering sound shook the house, and we knew it was the blowing up of the bridges, several explosions followed, and soon the bright flames leaped along the sides and floors of the bridges and illuminated the whole scene within the bounds of the horizon, the burning continued all night and our slumbers were disturbed with frequent explosions of gunpowder, placed under the two bridges. Robert went out with his gun and joined the guard which it was deemed proper to organise for the protection of the town against any stragglers or unruly persons who might chance to be prowling about. The first thing I heard this morning was that my two servants Martha and Susan had returned and requested permission to engage in their usual work. I went out feeling a good deal of indignation against them, but they seemed so humble and professed such penitence for having ever thought of going that I could only tell them that if they were willing to go to work again and content themselves in the condition in which God had placed them I would say nothing more to them about ever having gone.

SEPTEMBER 3RD

About 200 people came into town to-day from the surrounding country and general congratulations ensued. I was glad to receive from Richmond a sum of money which W sent me in May but which has never reached my hands until now. Some of our Cavalry rode into town this evening and were received with shouts of joy. The ladies lined the streets waving their handkerchiefs and chattering their welcome.

SEPTEMBER 4TH

Sent my portion of the soldier's breakfasts to Hazel Run by Julian and Sam. They came back with a great account of the way the soldiers were feasted on hot rolls beefsteak and coffee and their enjoyment of the good things after so long an abstinence. We attended Dr. Jno B Hall's[74] funeral yesterday evening and while standing around the grave the sound of the bugle and the tramp of cavalry horses fell upon our ears and very soon a troop of 700 horsemen appeared, they were our own "greys" we could have told it

The Mary Washington Monument was captured in its unfinished state during the Civil War. Mary was the mother of George Washington and a longtime Fredericksburg resident. Jane describes several walks to the monument in her journal. (*Library of Congress*)

by their gallant bearing if it had not been revealed by their dress, the air was rent with shouts, as we came home the streets were filled with excited people, and every body's face was lighted up with a glad smile. None of our own family have yet appeared and as we have not heard one word from them for two months we are somewhat anxious. We hope tomorrow will bring some news of them. Helen G and myself walked up to the Monument and had the pleasure of looking upon the green fields without the squads of Yankee pickets which have marred their beauty for many months past.

SEPTEMBER 5TH

Spent part of the morning making Confederate flags for my little boys, and seeing my friends and neighbours, some at their home, some at mine, all have their own tale to tell of suffering from the enemy and of gladness at the releif we are now enjoying.

A troop of our Cavalry crossed the river to-day near Knox's Mill and scoured the country beyond almost to the Potomac. They saw but few of the enemy, and all they did see they took prisoners and brought back to town. I expect the Yankees were very much surprised to find the river could be crossed at that point.

The 10th Va Cavalry came in this evening, so that we have a body of horsemen here now. We have heard nothing from our family yet.

SEPTEMBER 6TH

Mending clothes all the morning and in the evening walked out with Mrs. Cassel and Nannie Howison, enjoyed the walk very much, the absence of Yankee pickets greatly enhancing its pleasure.[75]

SEPTEMBER 7TH

Attended church which was very full, many of our citizens having already returned, exchanged greeting with many old friends as we came out, was surprised to see Mr. Horace Lacy among them, brother John's family dined with us, in the evening I went around to Sam's to take a note for Mr. John Ficklen to take to RRH in Richmond, and on my way back saw Mr. Broaddus who had just arrived, poor old gentleman he looked weather beaten after his long imprisonment.

SEPTEMBER 8TH

Commenced the day calmly but was soon thrown into a state of distressing excitement by my Son Robert coming in with the intelligence that he was compelled to go as a soldier[76] and I must get him ready to go by 2 o'clock on Tuesday. We were busily engaged with his shirts, when Reuben Gordon came, and we heard news of the army from him and of our friends in the upper country. He told us of the death of Dr. Jno Beale who was shot in his own yard in presence of his family by a party of marauders belonging to Pope's army. How long O Lord will the blood of our slaughtered people cry aloud for vengeance.

SEPTEMBER 9TH

Rose early to complete Robert's preparations for leaving as it was determined that he should go with Reuben Gordon and on to Orange Court House with Mr. Lacy. We hope that he may not be compelled to go farther than Richmond, as Mr. Lacy thinks he can get him a situation in G. W. Smith's division which is to be kept in Richmond for its defence. But it is by no means certain that he may not at once have to go into Maryland with the rest of the army and I parted from him with a heavy heart, every breath burthened with prayer to Almighty God for his preservation, soon after his departure I received a package of letters from my other absent ones and was comforted to learn that I should see my dear Minnie and John as soon as they could get means of conveyance. I was truly thankful that no serious misfortune had occurred to any of them in all this weary time, since we last heard. We have received our own as well as the Northern news, and learn that another great and decisive battle was fought on the 30th of August between Pope, and Lee, which resulted in the defeat of the former and his retreat to the immediate neighbourhood of Washington City, strange to tell the battle ground was the same old 'Manassas' where the first great battle was fought which resulted so disastrously to our enemies, I pray and hope that this may be the last. Our army has since gone into Maryland and threatens the north with the same devastating course which they meted out to us, but Oh that the northern Government may see the folly and madness of continuing this war and may at once make propositions of peace.

SEPTEMBER 10TH

I have been busy all day with my preparations for the school which is soon to commence, and I found constant occupation the best means of getting through this trying time, went to church this afternoon and heard "Charles White" deliver a short lecture from St. John's Epistle. Coming out saw Dickson White[77] who belongs to Braxton's Artillery was glad to learn that all our immediate friends in that company were well, and had so far escaped the dangers of the battle field, on my way home I called to see dear old Mrs. Hall, found her composed and serene, with her Consolation ever present. While I was sitting with her, one of the little girls brought me a letter from my dear John telling me of Minnie's arrival in Richmond and their expectation of coming home in a day or two, I have tried to make some arrangements for their conveyance from some point on the 'rail road' to Fred'g and hope it will not fail.

SEPTEMBER 11TH

Managed to get the bedstead taken down in the schoolroom and up stairs and most of Helen's furniture carried down to Mrs. Curtis', afterwards brother John came and brought a basket of fine peaches, he staid some time talking over the recent victories and their important results, especially their immediate results to Va. after he left we sewed vigorously until it was time to pare peaches for dinner and soon after dinner a friend sent us some late Richmond papers, and we pored over them until night, and felt great encouragement and thankfulness from all we read.

SEPTEMBER 12TH

Spent the day in making preparations for 2 Sabbaths, as we are to have services in the church on Saturday preparatory to the Sacrament on Sunday which is to be administered for the first time since Feb. last, after all the mending was done and clothes put away we took a walk across the fields and enjoyed the evening air and the sweet perfume of the meadows. On our return saw a gentleman who told me he had seen my dear Son William very recently in Columbus, Ga and I was so glad to hear from him.

SEPTEMBER 17TH

I have been made very happy since making my last entry, by the arrival of my children from Richmond they drove up in R Gordon's wagon on Monday and to my great joy Bob came back with them, they had a great many difficulties on the route and were until 3 o'clock Saturday night getting to Germanna from Gordonsville, but they are all well and very glad to get home. I have also received a letter from my son William in which he gives me hope of soon seeing him and this gives me great comfort tho' the sad vacuum remains in our midst and will never never be filled, the very fact of our being reunited makes us all feel more deeply the loss of our Charley, and my sorrow seems greater than ever.

The school commenced on Monday and we had 16 pupils, we they will be increased to 20 next week.

SEPTEMBER 18TH

To-day was appointed by the President as a Day of Thanksgiving for the victories which our armies have recently gained and the happy results which have followed. Mr. Lacy preached to a large congregation in the morning from the text, "The Lord hath done great things for us, whereof we are glad." In the discourse he gave us a short history of the summer campaign and it interested me very much to hear the glorious deeds of our armies under the noble commanders recited. There was service at the Baptist church in the afternoon, but we had dinner so late we could not attend, late in the evening, walked to the cemetery.

SEPTEMBER 25TH

This morning John and Robert left us for Richmond, they started at day break in a wagon for Beaver Dam on the Central RRd expecting to reach their destination tonight, it was very cold and a bleak wind was blowing and I fear they have suffered, but they told me this was no time for indulgence, and I need not fear they could take care of themselves.

Since writing last 'Jackson' has taken Harper's Ferry with 11,000 prisoners and a great many arms, and 'Lee' has fought and whipped the enemy in 'Maryland,' but was then obliged to cross the Potomac and return to Va as he had no supplies in Md.

OCTOBER 4TH

The week past has been spent in teaching school and writing letters, some of the family have been busy making under clothes for the soldiers as we have heard that the 30th Reg which was raised in this place, was very destitute, having lost all their clothes in the battle of Sharpsburg[78] (or as the Northern papers call it the battle of Antietam Creek). Our army returned into Va after this battle as they were unprepared for an advance into Pennsylvania and could not be sustained in that unfriendly part of Maryland, they are now encamped near Winchester.

OCTOBER 25TH

Willie arrived today and as his employment is at an end with Mr. A— for the present I hope he will be able to remain at home some time. We have a full school now and find our time fully occupied.

OCTOBER 28TH

Minnie left us this morning to return to school in N.C. and Mr. Brent[79] arrived at night to fill the vacuum caused by her absence, the latter came last from Tennessee as he has been with the army.

OCTOBER 31ST

William left us again to-day to take a position in Kent, Paine & Co's establishment in Richmond, his uncle Robert was kind in interesting himself to obtain this situation for him and he accepted it and went at once.

NOVEMBER 9TH

A company of Yankee cavalry[80] crossed the river at Falmouth this morning and dashed into town surprising our cavalry force here and capturing about 20 of them in the skirmish which occurred in the streets two men were killed one on each side, as soon as Capt. Simpson collected his forces on the outskirts of the town, he made an attack upon them put them to flight and many of the citizens joining in pelted them stones, one Yankee was knocked off his horse with a stone and taken prisoner. We spent the week after in anxiety and fear with continued reports of the enemy approaching our halcyon days were drawing to a close.

NOVEMBER 17TH

Our little army here was augmented by the arrival of a small force from Richmond. A considerable number of the enemy appeared above the town of Falmouth and

The upper part of Fredericksburg, including Jane Beale's neighborhood, as captured during the war. (*National Park Service*)

towards evening commenced firing upon our battery stationed in the field beyond White Plains.[81] Col. Ball[82] who was in command here returned the fire and there was an artillery duel kept up for about an hour. We watched the firing with intense interest until warned by the near approach of a shot we left our station at the window and came down stairs when we came into our front porch we found the whole neighborhood in a great state of excitement. The poor people from the upper part of the town had fled from their homes and were running wildly along with children in their arms, a shot had gone thro the paper factory and frightened the poor girls who were at work there terribly and they had joined the stampede, we yielded to the advice of the gentlemen of the neighbourhood and went to another part of the town until night came on when we returned home to await the events of another day, we learned then that the Yankees had got the range of our batteries and had disabled our guns killing one man and wounding several, one boy who had gone from curiosity to witness the fight had his foot shot and terribly shattered. Several horses were killed and the battery was withdrawn from the open field and hid behind the house at White Plains.

TUESDAY, NOVEMBER 18TH

Rose early and the first object that met my eyes upon looking out was a line of cavalry drawn up behind my schoolroom and stable, I soon learned they had been there

Union artillery on Stafford Heights, overlooking Fredericksburg. "Watched with trembling hearts the long line of Yankees pouring over the Stafford hills," Jane wrote on November 19, 1862. (*National Park Service*)

for hours and by a little concert of action among the neighbours we determined to give them their breakfasts and my boys and servants fed and watered fifteen by 9 o'clock. They were so grateful did my very heart good to give it to them. There was but little done in school today the children are so frightened and excited that it is almost impossible to do anything with them.

NOVEMBER 19TH

Watched with trembling hearts the long line of Yankees pouring over the Chatham hills to take the same station they occupied last summer, they come in countless numbers and our hearts sank within us as we thought of our little Spartan band who hold the fords, why do they remain to be sacrificed? And to bring destruction upon our town were queries that forced themselves upon us, nor did our wonder cease much when we heard Gen. Lee had telegraphed to Col. Ball "to hold the passage of the River at Fred'g at all hazards."

NOVEMBER 20TH

The rain poured in torrents all day and there was no cessation at night, anxiety kept me awake, and I was startled to hear knocks at both front and back doors simultaneously about midnight, upon enquiring who it was before opening the door the answer was "southern soldiers of McLaws' division who are fatigued from a long march are wet cold and hungry." I dressed myself hastily summoned Mr. Brent to my aid and got together every thing I could for the comfort of these poor fellows, I knew there was wood in my schoolroom ready for burning, I gave them the key, and filled a basket with bread, meat, molasses, milk, candles, matches, and gave them some pieces of carpet, pointed them the way and told them that was all I could do tonight but if they would stay in the morning I would give them some breakfast, and when I went out in the morning I found eleven had collected there, and there was a perfect lake of water had dropped from their clothes in the room where they had hung them. We now began to understand things, the army of Gen'l Lee was collecting around us and here a battle must take place ere long.

NOVEMBER 21ST

This day was spent in excitement and apprehension a demand was made for the surrender of the town by the Yankee Gen'l Burnside, which was answered by the military authorities now in possession, the subject was discussed thro' ambassadors all day, towards evening Gen'l Lee arrived and replied in person to Gen'l Burnside "If you want the town of Fred'g come and take it."[83]

NOVEMBER 22ND

The first news we hear in the morning is that the enemy will shell the town and we make hasty preparations to leave home. After many disappointments about a mode of conveyance we learn that Gen'l Lee has sent army wagons and ambulances into town to remove the women and children[84] and Mr. Brent secures an ambulance and then we begin to think where shall we go? Our preparations had all been made with a view of going to some empty house and almost everything was sent out to brother John's in the morning expecting to go from there, it was so late before we got off and having to go by Howison for our baggage detained us and threw out our plan—and so we determined to go out to the house of an acquaintance 'Mr. Ben Temple'[85] and ask shelter for the night, this was very unpleasant as we had not even the claim of friendly intercourse with the family never having exchanged visits with them, but the driver of the ambulance said he could only take us a few miles and my only strong inducement to go there was Mrs. Temple's large kind heart which I knew I could trust for a welcome and my confidence was well pleased for when we arrived at the gate tho' the house full of people she received us most kindly and told us we must stay and try and make ourselves comfortable, as she had just moved out that day and had nothing fixed.

NOVEMBER 29TH

Howison House.[86] We remained a week at Mr. Temple's and received much kindness, our army is all around us and we see soldiers by thousands every day, my son Julian has been ill for several days with fever which affects his brain and I feared to continue at Mr. Temple's as there was so much confusion around us it was impossible to have him nursed and I could not obtain proper medical advice, besides I knew we must be very much in the way at Berclair [Beauclair] and so determined to return to my brother's, where I can have Julian in a room to himself, but the house is crowded with soldiers and gentlemen from town and there is not much comfort.

NOVEMBER 30TH

To-day the girls came over from town with Mr. Brent and represented things as so quiet in town that it made me long to return to my own home with my sick boy as I know he would recover sooner there. I hear the soldiers also talking of the prospects and saying there will probably be no battle here as the Yankee General 'Burnside' will not risque it with the river behind him and our forces so advantageously placed. My daughters with Mr. Brent started to return to town about sunset, and met our

Battery boys[87] my four nephews Sam & Henry Thorburn and Jack and Ned Howison just on the brow of the hill, their Division having arrived in the neighborhood, they had obtained leave to come and spend the night with their friends. They turned back and we were soon all assembled in the back parlour making a cheerful group.

DECEMBER 6TH

Fredericksburg. We are at home once more and my sick boy is already improving, we have many comforts around us which it was impossible to obtain elsewhere and our good and faithful servants are ready to do any thing and every thing for our accommodation. We have but few neighbours left and feel as if we had the town almost to ourselves, I have been enabled to purchase wood, coal, meat, flour, and meal from one of my neighbours on very good terms and feel a comfortable assurance that we shall neither *starve* nor *freeze*.

SUNDAY DECEMBER 7TH

We spent the morning reading and conversing, I have Julian in my room and he sat up and listened with great interest to the Bible reading and an interesting book from the Sunday School Library. It is intensely cold and when the boys came up from their camp near Hamilton's Crossings, their hands were nearly frozen, we did our best to make them comfortable, they staid all night, and as we sat around our warm dining-room stove, talking cheerfully we could but contrast the scene in-doors with the howling of the bitter cold wind without,[88] the boys expressed fears that there would be *no battle here after all* as there was no sign of movement in the Yankee army and 'General Lee' had been heard to express doubts of Burnside's attempt to cross the river in the face of an army posted as our army was. All this made me feel more comfortable and assured, and yet it was a very awful and alarming thought that we lay down at night between two armies of 200,000 men at not more than a mile distant from us on either side and my only resource was to seek the 'Shadow of those Wings' which are ever extended over the helpless.

DECEMBER 8TH

The morning sun glowed so brilliantly thro' our open windows that it dispersed the sad fears and anxieties of the preceeding night and we rose to enjoy another one of 'God's blessed days.' After giving the boys breakfast and starting them to Camp with all the comforts they could carry, I set about putting my house in some order as we had been so uncertain of our stay that nothing but what was absolutely necessary for subsistence from day to day was attended to for some time, but if *Gen Lee* thinks an advance of the Yankee Army improbable, we may certainly feel *some right to home* again, with these thoughts I worked for several days feeling tolerably cheerful and hopeful as Julian was growing better every day, until a neighbour would come in to bid me 'goodbye' and tell me that I ought not to think of remaining here that they were going under the impression that every moment they remained was at a tremendous risque. And then when night would approach the same terrible apprehension of coming evil would oppress me, for I felt the responsibility of detaining my family consisting of my eldest daughter, Mr. and Mrs. Brent, and my two younger sons with myself and 3 servants in circumstances of danger. On the evening of the 10th our friends the two Mr. Lacys came in from the country to stay all night, they had put their horses at a neighbour's stable, but could find no place of refuge for themselves but our house, they expressed surprise to find us here and advised me to leave as they had heard in passing thro' our Army that there were indications of a speedy advance of the enemy, we sat around the fire conversing of the earthquake which had certainly been felt the night before, of the omens of coming evil which certain *ancient persons* had seen in the sky over the and of the terrible devastation to this country which even the presence of two such immense armies must cause, and of the probable terrors a coming rencontre. All this was not at all calculated to quiet our already excited nerves, and as I went up stairs to see if the room in which these gentlemen were to sleep was ready, I dropped the candlestick and sat down on the staircase in a perfect tremour, but I regained my composure when I took the Bible and sought the protection of Heaven for me and mine in prayer, and I went to sleep that night with the trust and confidence of a child in my heart.

DECEMBER 11TH

We were aroused before day by Gen Lee's 'Signal guns,' but not knowing their special significance,[89] we did not hurry ourselves, until 'Martha' our chamber maid came in and said in a rather mournful tone "Miss Jane the Yankees are coming, they have got two pontoons nearly across the river."[90] Before we were half dressed the heavy guns of the enemy began to pour their shot and shell upon our ill-fated town, and we hastily gathered our remaining garments, and rushed into our Basement for safety, on the first landing I remembered 'Julian' my sick boy and turned back to seek him. I met him with his youngest brother, half dressed with his clothes upon his arm, and tried to help him, but I was trembling so violently that I believe I was more indebted to him for assistance than he was to me. We sought the room often used for a kitchen, and as Susan made us a good fire (the fuel all being at hand), we

During the bombardment of Fredericksburg on December 11, 1862, Beale and her family huddled in their basement until nightfall. (*National Park Service*)

drew around it, with our hearts earnestly seeking the protection of Heaven. Our Pastor Mr. Lacy was still with us, and commenced in solemn but tender accents, repeating 'the 27th Psalm' as we all knew it we heartily responded to each verse. As the words "Tho an host should encamp against me, my heart shall not fear" were upon our lips, we startled from our seats by the crashing of glass and splintering of timber close beside us, and the first impulse was to rush to a dark closet near the wood-cellar, which occupying a central position, had no windows and presented two thick walls towards the firing but before I had moved half a doz steps, my youngest Son a boy of ten years, fell against me with the cry, "Oh Ma I'm struck," and by the aid of the candle light as I looked down, I saw that his sweet face was as white as the wall, I caught him in my arms and bore him along with me, and some one (I do not know who) helped me to take off his clothes, so that I might see the extent of the injury, he seemed to be stunned and helpless, but I soon saw that there was no terrible wound, only a deep redness of the skin about the shoulder and breast, we laid him down upon an old quilt, and when he came to himself, he told us he was sure something very heavy had struck him as it knocked him down and he had to crawl after us. Mr. Brent thought it was only a piece of brick displaced from the window set, but upon going back to the room in which we had been he found a twelve lb solid shot near where Sam stood, and this we have preserved as a memorial of his great danger and greater deliverance, the ball was no doubt very nearly spent before it reached the room in which we had taken refuge and the slight obstruction of the window sash *saved my boy's life*.[91] Strange to tell this incident, seemed to have some effect in composing my mind, and I sat down on a piece of wood with my poor *sick boy* on one side of me with his head resting upon a log and the wounded one on the other side both with fever and headache, poor 'Lucy' lay on some straw put down on the damp floor, almost paralyzed with terror, while Helen G sought refuge close under the wall on the side from whence the shots seemed to come. Mr. Brent and Mr. Lacy came back and forth between us and the other room, trying occasionally to speak a word of comfort to us but too evidently depressed themselves, to inspire us with the smallest amount of home. The servants ever mindful of our comfort got breakfast, of coffee, biscuits, and sausages and as every thing could be got without going out, they brought blankets and wrapped them around us and thus saved us from much of the bad effect which 13 hours spent on a damp cellar floor in mid winter would otherwise have produced.

About 1 o'clock there was a little cessation of the firing, and we heard my dear brother John's voice at the door calling us to come while we could get out of the town,[92] but when he came in and saw our condition he knew we could not walk, and get those poor sufferers past the danger in time, and after holding a hasty council with the other gentlemen it was judged too rash an undertaking for us to attempt then, brother John told us that the town was on fire in many places, a whole row of buildings on Main St were already burnt, and as my house had a shingled roof I thought we would soon be driven from it by fire also. Mr. Lacy left us with brother John and they could scarcely have got out of the town before the heavy Bombardment commenced again and the sound of 173 guns[93] echoed in our ears, the shrieking of those shells, like a host of angry fiends rushing through the air, the crashing of the balls through the roof and upper stories of the house, I shall never forget to the day of my death, the agony and terror of the next four hours, is burnt in on my memory as with hot iron, I could not *pray*, but only *cry* for mercy. About 6 o'clock the sound of my dear brother's voice was again heard at the door,[94] and now there was no time for parley, "come he said instantly, I have got an Ambulance for you, the enemy is across the river and there is not a moment to lose," we struggled to our feet wrapped the blankets we had over our heads and crept out of the cellar door into our yard blinded by the light, after being so long confined to darkness, I scarcely knew where I was, indeed the strange sight that met my first bewildered gaze, might well have astonished me, the palings were all down the yard was filled with armed men, the trees were cut off at their tops and their branches lay around impeding our progress. The Ambulance was drawn up behind the School House and we had to go through the whole length of the yard to get to it, some of the soldiers spoke to us and recommended haste as the enemy was coming up the hill not two squares off, our own men were evidently falling back, the town was to be given up to the enemy. We were shoved into the vehicle without much ceremony, and the horses dashed off at a speed that at another time woud have

Jane Beale and her family followed Hanover Street, shown at right in this wartime photo, when they fled town on the evening of December 11, 1862. (*National Park Service*)

alarmed me, but now seemed all too slow for our feverish impatience to be beyond the reach of those terrible shots which were still tearing through the streets of the town,[95] one struck a building just as we passed it, another tore up the ground a short distance from us. I was greatly distressed to leave the servants but they said they were not afraid of the enemy and would go over the river if they were in greater danger here. As we passed beyond the line of the town and the turn of the road put the 'Willis Hill' Promontory of land, between us and the firing, a sense of security came into my mind and deep and heartfelt thankfulness for our deliverance from this great evil, carried my spirit to the throne of Heaven in humble grateful prayer. But new objects attracted my attention and claimed my sympathy here, crowds of women and children had sought refuge in this sheltered spot and as night drew on they were in great distress, they could not return to the town which was already in possession of the enemy, and they had fled too hastily to bring with them the comforts even the necessaries of life. Some few had stretched blue yarn counterpanes or pieces of old carpet over sticks, stuck in the ground—and the little ones were huddled together under these tents, the women were weeping the children crying loudly, I saw one walking along with a baby in her arms and another little one not three years old clinging to her dress and crying "I want to go home." My heart ached for them and if I could I would have stopped the Ambulance and taken them in, but I did not know then that I might not have to spend the night out in the open air myself, the next scene that rose before us as we ascended the hill impressed me deeply with its gloomy grandeur looking back we beheld the town still on fire in many places, the old church steeples illuminated with the conflagration, 'Hazle Run Bridge' still burning and sending down great flakes of burning timber to the depths below, ever and anon thro' the clear evening air came the burst of the enemy's Artillery, the fire from the long line of guns on the Stafford hills could he easily discerned, they were still slowly firing over the devoted town, but even all this did not affect me as the sight of our soldiers did, we now came into their midst, drawn up along the hills in line of battle, great pine fires burning brightly and showing their stalwart forms and defiant faces as they looked towards the foe, "May God be with them, strengthening their hearts and arms for the coming struggle, and Oh give them the victory" broke from my heart in an almost frantic cry. But our spirited horses carried us swiftly through these scenes and presently turned off the 'Telegraph Road,' into the woods as we thought we would at least seek refuge in Mr. Temple's hospitable premises, and if the house was full he would let us stay in his barn, but when we drove up to the door the family rushed out and my dear friend Mrs. Temple carried me into the house almost in her arms, weeping as she went, at the idea of the dreadful peril to which we had been exposed all day. She gave up her most comfortable room for our accommodation and in a nice old-fashioned easy chair, before a blazing wood fire with my children around me, I ended the day so full of threatened danger and real horror in its beginning and its progress. I truly felt that praise for our deliverance was and ought to be the burthen of our song that night.

DECEMBER 12TH

The distant boom of cannon roused us early in the morning, and we thought of course the battle would be fought that day. Mr. Brent and the boys started for the

"Telegraph Road" to see and hear all that was going on and we wandered out over the hills and fields in the direction of the town for the same purpose, but feeling weak and weary I soon returned and helped Mrs. Temple about the housework as much as I could. The firing did not continue long except at distant intervals, and about noon they all came back and reported, the town filled with the enemy and a long line extending down the river as far as the eye could reach, Julian and Sam had seen some persons from the town who told them that the Yankees had sacked the town the night before and destroyed or bore away every article from the houses, that our house was burnt to the ground, and they had seen the servants at "Beverley Brooke's" this news filled us with the deepest sorrow here was my whole family thrown out in the world, homeless and utterly bereft of every comfort of life, and the future did look dark indeed, God's mercy kept us from despair in that trying hour, and caused us to cling to His promises. We tried to sustain each other with hope of what we might be able to do if we could get to North Carolina where we had near relatives, I had with me money enough to take us to Richmond and we thought my dear brother R might aid us there, we had no clothes but those we wore, no bonnets, no wrappings but the blankets we had around us when we fled from home.

DECEMBER 13TH

Again the booming of artillery sounded in our ears and this day there was but little cessation, all the gentleman and boys left us and hurried to the top of a high hill on my brother's farm which overlooked nearly the whole length of the battlefield, the river makes a considerable bend just at the town and within a few miles either way, from its banks enclosed by this bend there is almost a perfect level running back about a mile and a half, and this is again enclosed by an ampitheatre of hills, some rising into small mountains, our batteries were placed upon these hills, and the infantry were stationed at the foot of them about the centre of this ampitheatre, there projects into the plain, a Promontory of high hills at the base of which runs the road into the town, a stone wall encloses this road on either side, these hills are known now as 'Marye's Heights',[96] we were accustomed to call the promontory 'Willis Hill,' it was here the hottest of the battle raged on the left wing of Gen Lee's Army, tho there was terrible fighting on the right wing under Gen'l Jackson. It was a beautiful day, warm for the season and we were out among the hills all day listening with anxious hearts to the roar of Artillery sounding all along the extended line, 'Mrs. Temple' gave me the key basket and asked me to have some thing got for dinner and she went over to the road to get as near as she could to the scene of strife in which four of her sons were engaged, I was left almost alone my daughters went to a house where some of the wounded were brought, to try and do something to aid them, there were two sick men in a house in or near the yard, I went to see them and gave them milk and bread, got water and bathed their faces, they were exceedingly anxious to learn the progress of the battle, but I could not play "Rebecca" for them, the distance was too great and I was too old, and weary, and heartsick, to bear the sight of blood and carnage. One or two of the servants came back and gave me awful accounts of the scene on the road, the Ambulances of wounded men, the piles of amputated limbs already collecting in the corners of the yards at 'Mrs. Wiet's' and 'Goodwin's' but they could of course give me no idea of the real state of affairs. 'Aunt Sukey' got dinner ready and I set the table but no one came to dine, and I shut the doors of the dining room and went out towards the road feeling too anxious to remain in the house any longer I met my girls near the gate and the first glimpse I had of their faces alarmed me. There was such deep sadness, indeed a look of horror on their countenances, they said they had stayed as long as they could, but the sight of so much suffering and death had made them sick, that Gen'l Cobb[97] was killed and

The mother of General Thomas Reade Rootes Cobb grew up in this home, "Federal Hill," on Hanover Street. General Cobb died on the heights just west of his grandparent's home.

was laying at 'Mrs Wiet's' that Gen'l Cook[98] was severely wounded and was carried to Sunny Side,[99] that they heard that the Yankees and been repulsed five times in attempts to take "Marye's Heights" but that a great many of our men had fallen in defending it. I asked for the boys but they knew nothing of them, by the time we reached the house the sun was setting and judging that the whole party would now soon return and very hungry, having been all day without food I told Aunt Sukey to add biscuits and coffee to the dinner which was still on the table. One after another dropped in bringing each their own account, Mrs. Temple was comforted by hearing that her children were safe, only one was in the midst of the fight 'Skyron' [Skyren][100] belonging to "Braxton's Fred'g Battery" and he had so far escaped injury, my boys were also safe belonging to the same battery.

Mr. Brent and my little boys had witnessed the battle from the high hill, since called 'Lee's Hill,' from the fact that Gent Lee spent most of the day upon that commanding point. And they seemed deeply impressed with the scene, they had seen 'Meagher's Irish'[101] Brigade advance from the town, in full close columns and receive a storm of shell and shot from the Batteries stationed on Marye's Heights which thinned their ranks, and caused them to falter, but they returned to the charge with a bravery worthy of a better cause and hundreds of them who escaped the fire of the heavy guns fell beneath the shots of the infantry stationed along the stone wall, some within a hundred yards of the foot of the Heights. It is a fact worthy of remark that the field which was literally covered with their dead bodies, produced in 1847, the finest crop of corn ever raised in this section and that this crop or the greater part of it was sent as a donation to the starving Irish, and perhaps helped to feed some of these poor victims of the fight to-day. The field at the time I speak of belonged to Mr. Jno Spotswood Wellford and it was from him that the generous donation was sent. From all that could be gatherend by the reports of messengers from both right and left wings of the army, we knew that the enemy had been repulsed, but officers who came to Mr. Temple's said that but a small portion of our Army had been engaged in the fight, and they supposed that it would certainly be renewed on the morrow as the Yankees had such an immense army that they would be apt to try it again. Messengers were coming and going all night arrivals from the army below, some of the wounded brought here, kept us up pretty much all night, and in anticipation of a renewal of the fight, uncertain of its result and fearfully apprehensive of the loss of friends in a more general engagement, we could not sleep, but "we bitterly thought of the morrow."

Jane Beale and her family passed along this stretch of Sunken Road as they fled town. Two days later, Confederate infantry in the road would inflict a devastating defeat on Union troops in front of them. (*National Park Service*)

SUNDAY, DECEMBER 14TH

We heard a few guns in the morning and all the party dispersed to seek their positions of the day before, but the firing ceased presently and we heard of nothing more all that day and the next, but the moving of the wounded, the burying of the dead, various reports reached us one of which was that cars had arrived at Hamilton's Crossings filled with Campine Shot with which Genl Lee intended destroying the town and thus driving the Yankees from their place of refuge,[102] and this came upon me with a great shock of distress, as I had just heard from Mr. Brent that with the aid of a good Spy Glass, he thought he had ascertained beyond all doubt that my house was still standing, and hope had crept in of having a home once more. We afterwards heard that the known presence old and helpless females in the town, prevented our noble tender-heart General from availing himself of this advantage.

TUESDAY, DECEMBER 16TH

Early this morning a note and a messenger came from bro John, the note stated that during the night, the enemy had disappeared from our front and every man of them had gone across the river, every body was immediately in action, Mr. Brent and the boys started off to ascertain the condition of things in the town, and my daughters

The looting of Fredericksburg, 1862. The Beale House was not severely damaged, perhaps because one or more of her slaves remained in residence after the Beale's left. (*National Park Service*)

followed in the cart, hearing that hundreds of the dead were still lieing upon the battlefield through which we had to pass, I could not bear the trial, and sickened at the very thought, and so I remained at Berclair [Beauclair] and aided Mrs. Temple in nursing some poor sick and wounded men who had been brought there. Bernard Temple went in with Mr. Brent and the boys, and when I saw him returning in the evening, I ran out to hear his report, he told me that the town was in ruins and the streets filled with all sorts of articles which had been dragged from the houses, that he saw handsome mirrors, marbletopped tables crashed to pieces and tumbled amidst kitchen utensils, feather beds, piles of books all in the mud together,[103] but it was with strange and glad surprise that I heard that my house was apparently untouched,[104] there were numerous holes in the roofs and sides torn by the shells and balls but that the furniture was all in its place and that my servants had given them all a *good dinner* nicely served up with all the usual appendages, of plates, *spoons, knives & forks*, glasses, etc. I felt grateful very grateful for all this and wondered how it had happened, that I should have escaped so much better than any one else. ▪

Three Poems

Jane Beale hand-wrote these three poems in the final pages of her journal. They are presented here exactly as she wrote them.

THE WIFE

His house she enters, there to be a light
Shining within when all without is night;
A guardian angel o'er his life presiding,
Doubling his pleasures and his cares dividing;
Winning him back, when mingling in the throng,
From a vain world we love, alas! too long,
To fireside happiness and hours of ease,
Blest with that charm, the certainty to please,
How oft her eyes read his! her gentle mind
To all his wishes all his thoughts inclined;
Still subject—ever on the watch to borrow
Mirth of his mirth, and sorrow of his sorrow.

Your voiceless lips, O flowers! are living preachers
Each cup a pulpit, and each leaf a book
Supplying to my fancy numerous teachers
From lowliest nook.

All the jarring notes of life
Seem blending in a psalm
And all the angles of its strife
Slow rounding into calm.

That care and trial seem at last
Through memory's sunset air
Like mountain ranges overpast
In purple distance fair.

Endnotes

1. Journal entry for January 21, 1851.

2. Journal entry for August 30, 1850.

3. Journal entry for September 12, 1850.

4. Journal entry for May 14, 1862.

5. Journal entry for September 3, 1850.

6. Mrs. Sterling was Jane Beale's sister, Marion (1812–1868). Her husband, Richard Sterling, was a Princeton graduate who got a position teaching natural philosophy and chemistry at Hampden-Sydney College in Prince Edward County, Virginia, in 1848 at the age of thirty-six.

7. Jane Beale's mother was Helen Moore Howison (1784–1850), daughter of Edward Moore of Falmouth. Jane Beale's parents lived at the St. James House at 1300 Charles Street in Fredericksburg.

8. The home occupied by Jane and William Beale at 307 Lewis Street was built in 1816 by Garret Minor, leading citizen and mayor of Fredericksburg. The Beales purchased the home in 1846 for $3,500. Here Jane lived until her death in 1882. The front porch, attic window, and Gothic-styled window mullions were added after the house was sold by Jane's descendents in 1882 at a price of $2,500.

9. Jane Beale's beloved husband was William Churchill Beale (1791–1850), the son of William and Hannah Gordon Beale of Fauquier County.

10. V. Knox was Virginia Knox, wife of Dr. Thomas Knox. The Knox family lived at 1201 Princess Anne Street. In 1857 they moved across the street to 1200 Princess Anne Street, a parcel adjoining the Beale property. Mrs. Bankhead was the wife of Dr. William Bankhead and lived at 1116 Prince Edward Street in the "Steamboat House." Actress Tallulah Bankhead is descended from this same Bankhead family of Virginia.

11. Professor John White Webster was hanged for the grisly murder of Dr. George Parkman, a fellow professor at Harvard. The newspapers were filled with reports of the trial and Webster's sensational confession.

12. Lucy Cooke was the second daughter of Jane Beale. She was probably named after William Beale's sister, Lucy, who married Virginia author John Esten Cooke.

13. The sister in Albemarle was a half-sister, Eliza or Mary. They were the daughters of Jane's deceased husband William C. Beale and his first wife, Susan Vowles.

14. John Howison (1809–1879) was Jane Beale's older brother.

15. Sam Howison (1825–1885) was Jane Beale's youngest brother.

16. Sister Nannie was the wife of John Howison, Jane's older brother.

17. Willie and Johnnie were Jane Beale's two sons who had gone to stay with her sister Marion Sterling.

18. Miss Kitty and Miss Ellen Lomax were sisters of Judge John Tayloe Lomax, a distinguished lawyer and judge. Kitty Lomax lived at 1200 Princess Anne Street, the home built by, and shared with, her sister, Miss Rebecca Lomax. All three Lomax daughters, Kitty, Ellen, and Rebecca, remained unmarried throughout their lives. Their brother, Judge John Lomax, lived at 501 Hanover Street in Fredericksburg. The diary of their sister-in-law, Elizabeth Lindsay Lomax, was published in 1943 (see *Leaves from an Old Washington Diary, 1854–1863*. Elizabeth Lyndsay Lomax, edited by Lyndsay Lomax Wood. New York: E. P Dutton & Co.). The diary contains an abundance of information on Judge Lomax and the Lomax family in Fredericksburg.

19. G. Douglass Beale was the eldest son of Jane's husband William Beale and his first wife. Douglass died in April of 1857, at the age of twenty-eight, in Orange County, Virginia, at the home of his brother-in-law, Reuben Gordon.

20. Mr. George McPhail succeeded Samuel Wilson as minister of the Presbyterian Church. He served from 1842 to 1854.

21. The father of Jane Beale was Samuel Howison (1779–1845), who lived at the St. James House, one block from Jane's home.

22. Mattie T. was the daughter of Jane Beale's sister, Helen Thorburn (1817–1855).

23. Helen was Jane Beale's sister, Helen Howison Thorburn.

24. Jane Beale's eldest daughter was Helen Gordon Beale.

25. Miss Ellen Carmichael was the daughter of Dr. James and Elizabeth Carmichael. They lived at 309 Hanover Street in Fredericksburg.

26. The other brother who had been in Stockton, California, was Samuel Howison.

27. The Reverend Edward McGuire (1793–1858) was rector of St. George's Episcopal Church for forty-three years (1815–1858). He married the granddaughter of Fielding Lewis, Judith Carter Lewis, and they lived at 1100 Charles Street in Fredericksburg.

28. Miss Nannie F—was Ann Ficklen.

29. Brother Edward Beale was her husband's brother Edward Beale (1799–1878).

30. Mr. Joseph Nax was born in Germany in 1810. He moved to Fredericksburg with his wife, son, and two daughters in the 1840s. In 1859 Nax moved to Culpeper to become professor of music at the Culpeper Female Institute.

31. James H. Lawrence advertised his services in the local newspapers as a "Surgeon Dentist." He charged his patents a per tooth fee of fifty cents for fillings.

32. Mrs. John Lawrence Marye lived at "Brompton."

33. At this time, John Howison lived at "Rose Hill," now 1203 William Street, just west of what is today the University of Mary Washington campus in Fredericksburg.

34. The Plank Road was the Fredericksburg and Valley Plank Road, often called the Orange Plank Road. The road was finished in the 1850s as far as Orange Court House and was constructed of wooden planks made of oak or pine, each eight feet long by seven to twelve inches wide and four inches thick. These planks were placed over wooden stringers (also called sills) eight feet long by five inches wide embedded in the earthen road surface to create a stable platform. The Turnpike Act of 1817 mandated that wagon traffic drive on the right side of the road, leaving the left side open for lighter wagons to pass by those traveling slower due to heavier loads. This practice continues today.

35. Jane Beale's brother Samuel married Ann Ficklen.

36. As mentioned in Endnote 6, Jane's brother-in-law Richard Sterling began teaching chemistry and natural philosophy at Hampton-Sydney College in 1848. In December 1850, Sterling resigned from the college. The school investigated the

causes of the resignation but did not find the college at fault. Subsequently, Professor Sterling accepted the position of principal of the Edgeworth Female Seminary, and the family moved to Greensboro, North Carolina. Two of their sons, Edward and Neil, died while serving in the Confederate Army during the Civil War.

37. Jane's brother, Robert Reid Howison (1820–1906), earned a bright reputation as a historian with titles published across nearly a half-century. His important two-volume work on Virginia, one of the first of real merit, established Howison's credentials: *A History of Virginia, from its Discovery and Settlement by Europeans to the Present Time* (Philadelphia, 1846–1848). During the Civil War, Howison published a series of lengthy articles in *Southern Literary Messenger*, designed as a contemporary history of the Confederate cause. He also wrote *God and Creation* (Richmond, 1883), a thick (578 pages) religious discourse; and the even more voluminous *A History of the United States of America* (Richmond, 1892).

In August 1865, Howison addressed a long, fawning plea for mercy to the triumphant Yankees, boasting that he had performed no military duty except what was required by a controlling power. ("Applications of Former Confederates for Presidential Pardons," M1003, National Archives.) He narrowly survived the Richmond Capitol disaster in April 1870, being "severely bruised about the body."

R. R. Howison's history of the city of Fredericksburg, though virtually unknown because of its scarcity, contains much of genuine value, and of course benefits from the perspective afforded by its early date. *Fredericksburg: Past, Present and Future . . . Published under the Direction and for Benefit of the Fredericksburg Library and Lyceum Association* (Fredericksburg: Printed and Published by Rufus B. Merchant, 1880), contains fifty-two pages of fine type, and appeared in two variant wraps—light green and brown. The even-rarer second edition (the Virginia State Library does not even report a copy) omits the library and lyceum connection. *Fredericksburg: Past, Present and Future, New Edition with Supplement . . .* (Fredericksburg: J. Willard Adams, Publisher, 1898). The 1898 edition includes eighty pages, covered with pale yellow wraps. In 1880, Howison reveled in Fredericksburg's quiet culture and style and decried talk of chasing money; by 1898 he had repented of that rustic sentiment and gloried in development and prosperity.

38. Jane's husband William bought the Thistle Flour Mill in Falmouth in 1825 from James Vass, also the previous owner of the brick Falmouth dwelling that the Beale's called home before moving to Fredericksburg. To settle William's estate upon his death, the mill was sold in 1851 to Falmouth resident Duff Green, who renamed it the Eagle Mill.

39. The April 23, 1850 edition of the *Fredericksburg News* stated that Calhoun's coffin arrived by steamboat from Washington to Aquia Creek where it was met by a delegation of public officials from Fredericksburg. The coffin was transferred from the steamboat to a railroad car that stopped in Fredericksburg on its way to Richmond. "On the arrival of the train, it was met by a crowd of citizens who remained uncovered during the passage. A feeling of deep regret was marked in the countenance of all: citizens of every class and shade of politics collected at the depot to pay their last homage to the remains of one long a warrior, not in the ensanguined battle field, but the conflicts to extend liberty, and to defend the rights and constitution of his country. At 12 o'clock, minute guns commenced firing and the bells of all the churches tolled solemnly."

40. The Marye family lived at "Brompton," now the home of the president of the University of Mary Washington. John Lawrence Marye (1795–1868) bought "Brompton" in 1821 and greatly enlarged the house.

41. The home of Jane's brother John still stands today, located just off Lafayette Boulevard on Lee Drive within the Fredericksburg and Spotsylvania National Military Park. At the center of the farm sat the large, capacious Howison House, a circa 1859 two-and-a-half story Greek Revival-style brick dwelling with a two-story dependency connected to the main dwelling by a large one-and-a-half story brick hyphen. In 1876, Jane's brother sold his six-hundred-acre farm to his brother Robert Reid Howison, who named the property "Braehead" after the family home in Scotland. The property remained in the Howison family until 2006, when the house and remaining eighteen surrounding acres were sold to the Central Virginia Battlefield Trust, who placed historical easements on the property. Now protected, the trust resold the property to a private buyer in 2009.

42. Hazeldean was Hazel Run Valley located behind the National Cemetery on Lafayette Boulevard.

43. Jane's sons Charles Dornin Beale and John Howison Beale belonged to the elite Richmond City Guard, a company formed in December 1860 in response to the looming danger of war. The Guard became Company B of the 1st Virginia Infantry Regiment when mustered into Confederate service a few days after Virginia seceded.

The company commander, Captain James Kendall Lee (1829–1861), enjoyed a high military reputation as the war began, because he had published a popular military guide: *The Volunteer's Handbook: Containing an Abridgment of Hardee's Infantry Tactics, Adapted to the Use of the Percussion Musket. . . .* Lee's handbook quickly went through five editions, the fourth of which announced itself as launching the "Twenty-fifth thousand" copy. Although Jane did not mention it, and probably did not know the facts, Captain Lee had been mortally wounded at the head of the company five days before her July 23 entry, in a fight preliminary to First Manassas at Blackburn's Ford. Although her summary of the battle confused a few facts, it generally reported events more accurately than usual in contemporary civilian diaries.

John Howison Beale spent time in Richmond's Chimborazo Hospital early in 1862, and eventually was discharged because of poor eyesight. In 1863 he solicited a clerkship in the Confederate Treasury Department.

44. The Army of the Potomac was the official designation of the Confederate Army under Beauregard and Johnston in Northern Virginia. For most of the war this name was used by the Federal Army operating in Virginia.

45. Another Fredericksburg diarist identified the South Carolina horsemen as part of Wade Hampton's command.

46. Reuben Gordon was married to Eliza Beale, Jane Beale's stepdaughter.

47. Helen G. was Jane Beale's oldest daughter.

48. Helen's uncle at Bealton Station was John Beale.

49. Bealton Station on the Orange and Alexandria Railroad is now the community of Bealton, southeast of Warrenton on Route 17 in Fauquier County.

50. The Reverend Beverley Tucker Lacy (1819–1900), brother of Chatham's owner J. Horace Lacy, served early in the war as a supply pastor in Fredericksburg. He became the favorite preacher of the intensely devout Presbyterian Stonewall Jackson, and spent months in the field as a supernumerary on the general's staff. The

headquarters entourage around Jackson enjoyed Lacy's drollery, but some of them thought him not very pious and something of a fraud. Lacy was named after his father's best friend, Judge Beverley Tucker. Frequently, the third "e" in "Beverley" was dropped, sometimes even by Lacy himself.

51. New Orleans was captured on April 25, 1862.

52. Apparently Jane stayed so completely indoors that she did not observe the large cavalcade of Federal officers and accompanying horsemen who rode through town on Caroline and Princess Anne Streets on this date. This was the first major occupation of Fredericksburg, made possible by completion of pontoon bridges across the Rappahannock River.

53. Jane's eldest son, William Coalter Beale, lived in Apalachicola, Florida, in 1861, but returned home to defend Virginia and joined the Fredericksburg Artillery on August 1. He was promoted to corporal that fall and to sergeant in April 1862. William's youthful first cousin, Edward Moore "Ned" Howison (1846–1864), volunteered as a substitute to take William's place in the Fredericksburg Artillery. Ned paid a dreadful price for his family fealty, dying in battle at Ream's Station below Petersburg on August 21, 1864, while still in his teens. Ned's brother John Hancock Howison (b. 1844) had joined the battery from the start. John, too, died in his teens, at Gettysburg.

54. Jane's heart-wrenching ordeal at the death of her son, which went on for two weeks as a result of false hopes based on false reports, was in vain from the start. The early and highly reliable history of the 1st Virginia, by a sergeant who served in the regiment, lists Charley as "killed"—not mortally wounded. The company clerk also reported Charley "killed" outright in the final muster roll that includes his name. So did casualty enumerations printed in both the *Richmond Dispatch* and *Whig* just four days after the battle.

Many of the 1st's casualties at Williamsburg on May 5 came at a crucial moment when the unit charged a Yankee battery. Arguments between veterans of the 1st and those of the 9th Alabama, over who deserved credit for the capture, raged on long after the war. Charley is buried in Section 8 of the Fredericksburg City Cemetery.

55. Archibald Alexander Hodge was pastor of the Presbyterian Church from 1855 to April 1861. His ties were with the North, and he left to become a professor at Princeton University.

56. Mr. William F. Broaddus (1801–1876) was pastor of the Fredericksburg Baptist Church from 1853 to 1862 and lived at 1106 Princess Anne Street. He was one of nineteen prominent Fredericksburg men arrested by the Federals in August 1862.

57. General Marsena Rudolph Patrick (1811–1888) served as provost marshal of Fredericksburg and environs for the occupying enemy army. He administered martial law firmly but without any malice or rancor, and actually managed to earn the grudging admiration of the townspeople. Not surprisingly, he was cashiered for the crime of excessive civility to Southern civilians within his power.

58. Logan Sims Robins (1841–1912) had only been a lieutenant for a fortnight when he fought as a subaltern in Charley's company at Williamsburg. Robins survived a wound at Frayser's Farm that summer, and Yankee captivity in 1865, to live into the twentieth century.

59. Sister Nanny was Samuel Howison's wife, Jane's sister-in-law.

60. The departure of a large force from Fredericksburg was the result of the success of General Stonewall Jackson's campaign in the Shenandoah Valley.

61. The rumored Hanover fight was the Battle of Slash Church (also called Hanover Court House) on May 27. Neither side gained a marked advantage, but the action launched several weeks of violent and important fighting around Richmond.

62. Jane's entry refers to the Battle of Seven Pines on May 31 and June 1. In its aftermath, General Robert E. Lee took command of the army he would make famous, starting with the Seven Days Campaign around Richmond, which repulsed Yankees from within sight of the Capitol. Jane's entries in late June and early July comment on that weeklong campaign.

63. In June 1862 the military governor was Brigadier General John F. Reynolds of Pennsylvania, who was killed later at Gettysburg.

64. Mr. Horace Lacy was the brother of the Reverend B. T. Lacy and a major in the Confederate Army. His wife was Betty Churchill Jones. Their homes were "Chatham" in Stafford County just across the river from Fredericksburg, "Greenwood" in Spotsylvania County, and "Ellwood" in Orange County.

65. Aunt Eva Young was a free Negro emancipated by Jane Beale's grandfather, Edward Moore. She was listed as a member of Jane's household in the 1850 U.S.

Census and was fifty years old then. During the 1850s, many free Negroes from Fredericksburg went to Chicago to live.

66. Jane's dismay about loss of Generals Joseph E. Johnston and Gustavus W. Smith reflected casual, and predictably inaccurate, understanding of events based on reading newspapers. By almost any rational standard, removal of both men from command positions redounded to the benefit of Southern armed forces.

67. Mrs. Walker Peyton Conway (1807–1891) had probably been visiting her son, Moncure Daniel Conway (1832–1907), who at that time was editor of the newspaper *Commonwealth* in Boston. His well-known antislavery views could have been the reason for Jane Beale's remarks about Mrs. Conway.

68. The Battle of Fredericksburg drove Samuel Rodgers (1824–1894) away from town as a refugee. He wound up in the Kanawha Valley, where he became chaplain of the 22nd Virginia Infantry, whose commander was George S. Patton, a native of Caroline Street in Fredericksburg; perhaps the local connection led to his appointment. Although Jane spelled his surname without the "d," and so did Jack Johnson in his history of the local church, Rodgers's official Compiled Service Record from the war used Rodgers. So did his obituary in the *Winchester Times*. Rodgers came back to the Fredericksburg Methodist Church in the 1880s.

69. This was probably Miss Mary Cady who married financier Jonathan Sturges of New York and whose daughter married J. Pierpont Morgan.

70. In total, nineteen Fredericksburg men were taken hostage: Reverend William F. Broaddus, James McGuire, Charles C. Wellford, Thomas F. Knox, Beverley T. Gill, James H. Bradley, Thomas B. Barton, Benjamin Temple, Lewis Wrenn, Michael Ames, John Coakley, John H. Roberts, John J. Berrey, Dr. James Cooke, John F. Scott, Montgomery Slaughter, George H. C. Rowe, William H. Norton, and Abraham Cox. The arrests were the result of a series of harsh new edicts promulgated the previous week by the new Federal commanding general, John Pope. Pope drew the hatred and scorn of Southerners because of his orders directing the molestation of civilians. General Lee went on record as being anxious to "suppress" Pope.

71. Jane's remarks concern the battle in Culpeper County that more usually is called Cedar Mountain than Slaughter Mountain. Stonewall Jackson thoroughly defeated a Federal advance guard of General John Pope's army, commanded by General Nathaniel P. Banks, there on August 9. Cedar Mountain was Jackson's last independent command of a battlefield.

72. "Somervilla" was the country home in Culpeper County of Fredericksburg merchant James Somerville (1777–1858) and his wife Mary Atwell Somerville (1778–1845). The Somerville's were cousins of the Howison family.

73. Evidently not all of the ladies were able to repress the exaltation that they felt at the Federal retreat, because one of the departing officers was prompted to express the sentiment that "The worst part of a retreat is to see the women look so damned happy at our departure."

74. Dr. John B. Hall was the owner of Hall's Drug Store located at the northwest corner of William and Caroline Streets. He lived in what is today known as the Stephenson-Doggett House at the northwest corner of Princess Anne and Amelia Streets in Fredericksburg.

75. Jane's remarkable accuracy in identifying people and units, by the standards of female civilian diaries, continues in this entry. The 10th Virginia Cavalry only paused briefly in Fredericksburg while marching toward the Potomac from Hanover Court House. By September 11, the regiment had ridden through Catlett's and Haymarket to Leesburg and thence to Winchester.

76. Robert Cecil Beale had enlisted in the Fredericksburg Artillery, where his brothers John and William also served, in March 1862, and drew a $50 bounty. The date suggests that he was driven to enlistment by the new conscription acts. Why he then went out of service with the battery within a few months is not of record. After being drafted in September 1862 and assigned to the 25th Virginia Infantry Battalion ("the City Battalion"), a somewhat irregular Local Defense Troops unit, Robert transferred back to join friends and family in the Fredericksburg Artillery on May 6, 1863, as assigned by Special Orders No. 109/3 from the Adjutant and Inspector General's Office. He served steadily with the battery until paroled at Appomattox.

Dr. Beale's murder was one of an astonishing flood of murder, rape, and other violent crimes against civilians by Yankee marauders in Virginia. Although many, probably most, of them of course escaped punishment, records of some eighty-three thousand trials by Federal courts survive, nearly two thousand of them for rape or murder.

77. John Dickson White, a wealthy Pennsylvania-born silversmith in Fredericksburg, joined the Fredericksburg Artillery in 1862. He transferred to ordnance duty in Richmond in December 1862, no doubt to take advantage of his metallurgical skills. White died in 1864. Braxton's Artillery was the Fredericksburg Artillery, originally

commanded by Captain Carter Moore Braxton (1836–1898), "a splendid officer and gentleman." Subsequent captains, for whom the unit was informally named during their command tenures, were Edward Avenmore Marye (1835–1864) and John Gray Pollock (1832–1906).

78. More men from Fredericksburg and the adjacent counties served in the 30th Virginia Infantry than in any other Confederate infantry unit. Three of the 30th's ten companies came primarily from the city; one from Spotsylvania; four from Caroline; and one each from King George and Stafford. The 30th suffered dreadful casualties on September 17, 1862, around the famous Dunkard Church at Sharpsburg, or Antietam. Its loss of nearly two hundred men there in a few minutes came close to equaling all of the 30th's casualties for the rest of the war combined.

79. Mr. John C. Brent, from Paris, Kentucky, married Jane Beale's daughter, Lucy Cooke Beale.

80. The dash by Yankee cavalry into the streets of town on November 9 did not accomplish much, nor have any lasting impact. It proved a thrilling episode for the townspeople, though, as the city's women ran onto their porches and waved hand-kerchiefs in support of the Southern cavalrymen who repulsed the raiders. Yankee horsemen from Indiana and Ohio surprised the 15th Virginia Cavalry, made up mostly of Northern Neck troopers, which was quartered in town.

Ulric Dahlgren, who led the attackers, became famous or infamous, depending on one's perspective, for a much more substantial raid launched toward Richmond in February 1864, intended to murder President Davis and cabinet members. Members of the Fredericksburg-area's 9th Virginia Cavalry eventually cornered Dahlgren and killed him in King and Queen County on March 2. That later unrelated event came to be renowned as "Dahlgren's Raid," not to be confused with the brief incursion into Fredericksburg's streets in November 1862.

Scottish-born Captain James Forbes Simpson (1827–1868) commanded a company of the 15th Virginia Cavalry that played a role in repulsing the Fredericksburg raid. The ladies of town presented a flag to Simpson in appreciation of his company's endeavors on their behalf.

81. "White Plains" was located in the vicinity of Princess Anne Street and Virginia Avenue.

82. Colonel William Bernard Ball (1816–1872) commander of the 15th Virginia Cavalry, was the senior Confederate present. Within a few hours, dozens of officers of higher rank would arrive in or near town.

83. The communication with General Burnside actually was signed by Mayor Montgomery Slaughter after checking with the very recently arrived General Lee. Slaughters's letter promised that their city would not be used for military purposes, but he passed on Lee's warning "that, while their [Confederate] troops will not occupy the town, they will not permit yours to do so."

84. In one instance, Lee dispatched troopers from his own entourage to assist a family with numerous children. The multitude of eyewitness accounts of the battle written by Confederate participants almost invariably include mention of some particularly heart-rending scene connected with the exodus.

85. Ben Temple lived at "Beauclair," located on Harrison Road west of its intersection with Jefferson Davis Highway.

86. A description of the Howison House, now known as "Braehead," is provided in Endnote 41. Of specific interest to Jane's journal entry for November 29, 1862, General Robert E. Lee was a breakfast guest at John Howison's home before the Battle of Fredericksburg in December of that year. In 1864, uninvited Union troops vandalized the house; several reminders including graffiti can still be noted in the house today.

87. The four young men in "our Battery" all belonged to the Fredericksburg Artillery, attached at this time to A. P. Hill's division. The Battery fought from a position south of Deep Run and Lansdowne Road, near Bernard's Cabins. Jane's nephews John and Ned Howison have appeared earlier. Henry Clay Thorburn (1840–1898) survived the war and is buried near John Howison in the Fredericksburg City Cemetery. Samuel H. Thorburn (b. 1839) lived in Apalachicola, Florida, in 1861, as did Jane's eldest son William. Samuel survived the war and married in Chesterfield County in 1866.

88. On December 6 there were four inches of snow on the ground and the temperature had dropped low.

89. The signal guns were two shots in succession fired by Captain P. W. Read's Georgia Battery from the hilltop just behind "Braehead." The signal guns came just

before 5 a.m. Before that time, an effort had been made to alert the civilians still in town to their mortal danger. Lieutenant Colonel John G. Fizer, of the 17th Mississippi Infantry, had been positioned by General William Barksdale along the west bank of the Rappahannock from a point north of Hawke Street south beyond the lower end of the city. Fizer later reported his efforts to clear noncombatants from the dangerous area: "Knowing there were many families occupying the houses on the margin of the river, I deemed it proper to notify all the women and children of their danger and give them time to get from under the range of the enemy's guns." Apparently, Jane Beale's household was overlooked, or else Colonel Fisher did not extend his warning so far back from the river as three streets.

90. The artillery fire that interrupted the Beales was that of the six six-gun batteries brought to the verge of the river in the vain effort to dislodge the Mississippi riflemen.

91. Evidently a stray shot crashed into the basement and resulted in the wounding of Samuel Howison Beale by debris. The recovery of a twelve-pounder shot would seem to identify the source of the trouble, although the fortunate young man was surely hit only by some building material dislodged by the ball.

92. The temporary interlude during which John Howison came to his sister's aid was after the period of heavy concentrated fire on the nonmilitary portion of the city. The renewed bombardment was accompaniment to further direct efforts to bridge the river.

93. Jane Beale's reference to a precise "173" guns is evidence that this particular entry was made at least slightly after the event. She could hardly have had so concrete an estimate on December 11. The estimate is quite close to the truth, although a bit high.

94. It must have been at about 4:30 p.m. that the harried inhabitants of the Beale house made their dash for safety. The timing coincides with the military situations as outlined by Jane Beale and by the circumstances surrounding the flight. Her own estimate that it was 6 o'clock is obviously far too late, since she was "blinded by light." Sunset in Richmond on December 11, 1862, was at 4:56 p.m.

95. The route followed by the ambulance carrying the Beale family must have been west on Hanover Street or some parallel street, then across the Sunken Road, which was to become so dreadfully famous within a few hours, then around the southern edge of what is now called Marye's Heights and on out Telegraph Road (now Lafayette Boulevard, U.S. Route 1). Jane mentions turning behind the shelter

of the Willis Hill promontory. This would be at the point where the ambulance left the Sunken Road and turned into the rather deep valley of Hazel Run. Before the war, the heights, now owned by the National Park Service and occupied by the National Cemetery, were known as Willis Hill because of their long occupancy by the Willis family. The extension of the same ridge to the north to Hanover Street was Marye's Hill or Heights. Apparently the national prominence gained by the ridge during the battle resulted in the extension of the name "Marye's Heights" to the whole area, based on the distinguishable Marye home, "Brompton."

96. Jane's comments along these lines in the December 13 entry are conclusive evidence of much later authorship of this portion of the diary.

97. General Thomas Reade Routes Cobb was a brilliant young Georgian lawyer and politician who had become a successful military man despite his lack of background in that field. He was wounded in the leg while commanding his brigade in the Sunken Road and bled to death shortly thereafter. Cobb's mother was a Rootes of Fredericksburg. The general was killed within sight of her home, "Federal Hill," where he had played during childhood Virginia summers.

98. Brigadier General John Rogers Cooke, the son of a Northern general and brother-in-law of legendary Confederate cavalryman J. E. B. Stuart, suffered a bullet wound to the head while commanding his men atop Willis Hill. He survived the dire wound and returned to lead his brigade in the battles west of Fredericksburg in 1864.

99. "Sunnyside" is located on Route 208 west of Four Mile Fork. During the Civil War, it was the home of Mrs. Betsy Barton French.

100. William Skyren Temple (1839–1904) served early in the war in the Fredericksburg Artillery, beside Jane's sons and their kinsmen. He supplied a substitute to escape service, but when subject to conscription later in the war he joined the Purcell Artillery and later the 9th Virginia Cavalry.

101. Meagher's Irish Brigade was one of many Federal brigades who climbed the sloping plain below Marye's Heights and was beaten back with consummate ease. Their recognizable uniforms made them stand out from the other waves of attackers.

102. It is impossible to find any substance in the rumor reported to Jane Beale that General Lee considered destroying the city. Lee's reaction to the Federal bombardment on the eleventh had been wrathful; he was overheard to say, "These people

delight to destroy the weak and those who can make no defense; it just suits them!" It has been widely noted that Lee's unwillingness to shell the Federals in the city cost him the opportunity to extract huge losses from his enemies and possibly create a military situation favorable enough to lead to a change in the tide of the war.

103. The desolation and destruction in Fredericksburg was the result of the bombardment of the eleventh and of the wanton sacking of the town that went on from the first Federal occupation until their departure on the night of the fifteenth. The Army of the Potomac was generally quite well mannered, considering the stresses incumbent on men fighting a bitter civil war, but at Fredericksburg the men got completely out of hand. Contemporary accounts, most of them from Federal troops, agree that the vandalism was widespread. The Provost Marshal General of the Army of the Potomac, incensed by the vandalism, rode through the streets flailing his riding whip against his troops. Later he carried some officers directly to General Hooker for disciplinary action.

104. There is no answer as to why the Beale House was relatively untouched by the destruction. There is the possibility that the presence of servants was sufficient to deflect the looters. The traditional explanation, expressed by Jane's two grandnieces who lived in the family home "Braehead" until the early 1980s, is that the house was spared as a result of the kindness shown Union troops who were allowed to rest in the shady yard and drink from the good well while the town was under occupation. ▪

Index